quick-method QUILTS WITH STYLE

LEISURE ARTS, INC.
LITTLE ROCK, ARKANSAS

EDITORIAL STAFF

Vice President and Editor-in-Chief:
   Anne Van Wagner Childs
Executive Director: Sandra Graham Case
Executive Editor: Susan Frantz Wiles
Publications Director: Carla Bentley
Creative Art Director: Gloria Bearden
Production Art Director: Melinda Stout

DESIGN
Design Director:
   Patricia Wallenfang Sowers
Senior Designer: Linda Diehl Tiano

PRODUCTION
Managing Editor: Sherry Taylor O'Connor
Technical Writers: Sherry Solida Ford,
   Kathleen Coughran Magee, and
   Barbara McClintock Vechik

EDITORIAL
Associate Editor: Linda L. Trimble
Senior Editorial Writer:
   Terri Leming Davidson
Editorial Writer: Robyn Sheffield-Edwards
Editorial Associates:
   Tammi Williamson Bradley and
   Darla Burdette Kelsay
Copy Editor: Laura Lee Weland

ART
Book/Magazine Art Director:
   Diane M. Hugo
Senior Production Artist:
   M. Katherine Yancey
Art Production Assistants: Brent Jones,
   Katie Murphy, Dana Vaughn, and
   Karen Wilson
Photography Stylists: Christina Tiano Myers,
   Sondra Daniel, Karen Smart Hall, and
   Aurora Huston

BUSINESS STAFF

Publisher: Bruce Akin
Vice President, Finance: Tom Siebenmorgen
Vice President, Retail Sales:
   Thomas L. Carlisle
Retail Sales Director: Richard Tignor
Vice President, Retail Marketing:
   Pam Stebbins
Retail Customer Services Director:
   Margaret Sweetin

General Merchandise Manager: Russ Barnett
Distribution Director: Ed M. Strackbein
**Executive Director of Marketing and
   Circulation:** Guy A. Crossley
Circulation Manager: Byron L. Taylor
Print Production Manager: Laura Lockhart
Print Production Coordinator:
   Nancy Reddick Baker

Library of Congress Catalog Number 95-81736
Hardcover ISBN 1-57486-017-8
Softcover ISBN 1-57486-018-6

INTRODUCTION

From traditionally rustic to playfully romantic, you'll find the perfect quilt patterns to reflect your taste when you have Quick-Method Quilts With Style *at your fingertips. Throughout our collection, you'll learn how to re-create patterns from yesteryear using the best of today's time-saving hints. Our contemporary original designs utilize the newest tools and techniques, too, so you can enjoy quilting your own heirlooms! You can even coordinate an entire room with matching pillows and other accessories. No matter if you're just starting out or you've been quilting for years, you'll see at a glance which projects are right for you, thanks to the helpful skill rating assigned to each of our quilts and wall hangings. With busy schedules in mind, we've also included a variety of unique fast-to-make designs, such as a mantel scarf, a padded trunk, and a bewitching centerpiece. So turn the page and begin accenting your decor with a style that says welcome, a style that says comfort, a style that says home — all with the timeless beauty of quilts!*

TABLE OF CONTENTS

TREE OF LIFE COLLECTION **8**

Tree of Life Quilt 12

Tree of Life Pillow 14

Delectable Mountains Doll Quilt 15

Kansas Troubles Pillow 17

STAR OF BETHLEHEM COLLECTION **18**

Star of Bethlehem Quilt 22

Star of Bethlehem Wall Hanging 27

Star of Bethlehem Pillow 29

Sawtooth Pillow 30

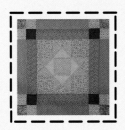

SQUARE DANCE **32**

Square Dance Quilt 34

FOUR SEASONS COLLECTION **38**

Four Seasons Quilt 42

Changing Seasons Wall Hanging 45

Appliquéd Clothing 47

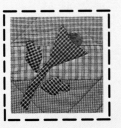

PLAID GARDEN..............................48
Plaid Garden Quilt..50

NINE-PATCH MANTEL SCARF......54
Nine-Patch Mantel Scarf 56

BASKET COLLECTION 58
Basket Quilt..62
Hope Chest with Padded Panel 64
Pretty Pincushion 64
Chatelaine...65
Basket with Padded Lid 66

TRUE HEART WALL HANGING....68
True Heart Wall Hanging..................................70

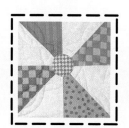

NURSERY RHYME CRIB SET 74

Nursery Rhyme Crib Quilt 78
Dust Ruffle 81
Pinwheel Chair Pad 81
Bumper Pads..82

PINEAPPLE QUILT 86

Pineapple Quilt 88

LITTLE QUILTS 92

LeMoyne Star Wall Hanging 96
Charm Doll Quilt 97

FLORAL NINE-PATCH.....................98

Floral Nine-Patch Quilt 100

HAUNTING COLLECTION...........102

Spooky Wall Hanging...104
Wanda Witch..104
"Trick-Or-Treat" Blocks 105

BACHELOR'S PUZZLE COLLECTION 108

Bachelor's Puzzle Quilt 112
Reversible Wall Hanging 115

STARRY PATH 118

Starry Path Quilt 120
Curtain Tiebacks 123

CHARMING DISHES COLLECTION......124

Broken Dishes Quilt 128
Charm Table Topper 129
Iris Wall Hanging 130

LADY OF THE LAKE COLLECTION......132

Lady of the Lake Quilt......136
Table Setting 139
Apron 140

GENERAL INSTRUCTIONS 142
CREDITS 160

TREE OF LIFE COLLECTION

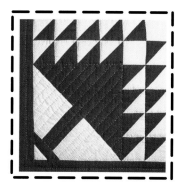

Adapted from the classic Pine Tree design, the Tree of Life is one of America's oldest patchwork patterns, dating back to early Colonial times. The design, like many of the day, received its name from Bible verses that referred to the tree found in Paradise. For our variation, we simplified the pattern by using plain setting triangles along the quilt's edge in place of the half blocks used in the antique model shown here. Making the blocks is fast and easy using grid-pieced triangle-squares, and solid edgings create an interesting contrast when set against basic sashing strips. Pair the quilt with our coordinating accessories for a collection that's blissful to create!

John Bunyan's novel Pilgrim's Progress *inspired another of our oldest quilt patterns. Early American settlers were especially captivated by a passage that described the beautiful landscape and "delectable mountains" awaiting the book's hero after he escaped oppression. Quilters of the day depicted the image as the picturesque block used for our miniature Delectable Mountains quilt (below). Made using triangle-squares and plain setting triangles, the quilt is a beautiful complement to the Tree of Life design and easily doubles as a table topper or doll quilt (shown on page 94). Complete the ensemble with attractive throw pillows (opposite) created from single quilt blocks.*

TREE OF LIFE QUILT

SKILL LEVEL: 1 2 3 4 5
BLOCK SIZE: 9¼" x 9¼"
QUILT SIZE: 69" x 86"

We simplified the piecing of this quilt by substituting solid setting triangles for the half blocks used on the edges of our antique quilt (see Assembly Diagram, page 14). We also resized the too-small quilt to fit a traditional twin-size bed.

YARDAGE REQUIREMENTS

Yardage is based on 45"w fabric.

4¾ yds of red solid
2⅝ yds of cream solid
2⅛ yds of green solid
5¼ yds for backing
1 yd for binding
81" x 96" batting

CUTTING OUT THE PIECES

All measurements include a ¼" seam allowance. Follow ***Rotary Cutting****, page 144, to cut fabric.*

1. **From red solid:**
   - Cut 2 strips 14⅜"w. From these strips, cut 4 squares 14⅜" x 14⅜". Cut squares twice diagonally to make 16 **setting triangles** (you will need 14 and have 2 left over).
   - Cut 3 strips 3¼"w. From these strips, cut 31 **sashing squares** 3¼" x 3¼".
   - Cut 16 strips 1½"w. From these strips, cut 32 **short inner borders** 1½" x 8¾" and 32 **long inner borders** 1½" x 9¾".
   - Cut 4 strips 1½"w. From these strips, cut 32 **trunks** 1½" x 4½".
   - Cut 1 strip 5⅛"w. From this strip, cut 5 squares 5⅛" x 5⅛". Cut squares twice diagonally to make 20 **sashing triangles** (you will need 18 and have 2 left over).
   - Cut 3 strips 6⅜"w. From these strips, cut 16 squares 6⅜" x 6⅜". Cut squares once diagonally to make 32 **triangles**.
   - Cut 2 strips 2"w. From these strips, cut 32 **squares** 2" x 2".
   - Cut 6 **rectangles** 15" x 20" for triangle-squares.
   - Cut 2 squares 7⅜" x 7⅜". Cut squares once diagonally to make 4 **corner setting triangles**.
2. **From cream solid:**
   - Cut 3 strips 1⅞"w. From these strips, cut 64 **squares** 1⅞" x 1⅞".
   - Cut 1 strip 1¼"w. From this strip, cut 32 **small squares** 1¼" x 1¼".
   - Cut 3 strips 6"w. From these strips, cut 16 squares 6" x 6". Cut squares twice diagonally to make 64 **triangles**.
   - Cut 6 **rectangles** 15" x 20" for triangle-squares.
3. **From green solid:**
   - Cut 20 strips 3¼"w. From these strips, cut 80 **sashing strips** 3¼" x 9¾".

ASSEMBLING THE QUILT TOP

Follow ***Piecing and Pressing****, page 146, to make quilt top.*

1. To make triangle-squares, place 1 red and 1 cream **rectangle** right sides together. Referring to **Fig. 1**, follow **Making Triangle-Squares**, page 147, to complete 96 **triangle-squares**. Repeat with remaining **rectangles** to make a total of 576 **triangle-squares**.

Fig. 1

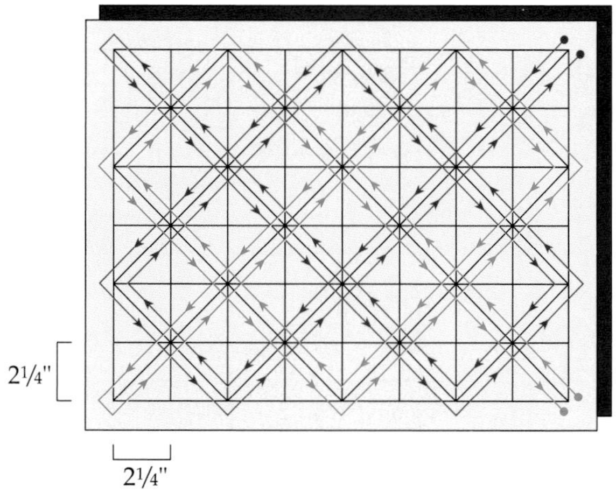

triangle-square (make 576)

2. Sew 10 **triangle-squares** and 2 **squares** together to make **Unit 1**. Make 32 **Unit 1's**.

Unit 1 (make 32)

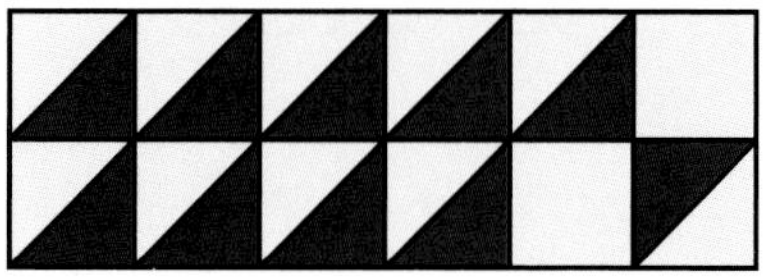

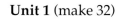

3. Sew 8 **triangle-squares** together to make **Unit 2**. Make 32 **Unit 2's**.

Unit 2 (make 32)

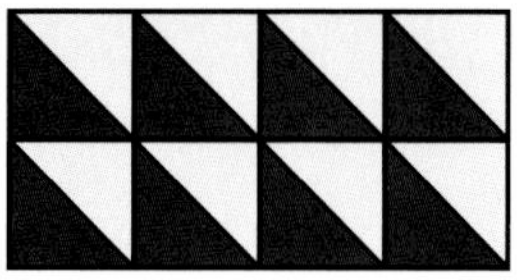

4. Sew 1 **triangle**, 1 **Unit 2**, and 1 **Unit 1** together to make **Unit 3**. Make 32 **Unit 3's**.

Unit 3 (make 32)

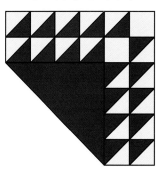

5. Referring to **Fig. 2**, sew 1 **trunk** and 2 **triangles** together. Trim trunk even with triangles to make **Unit 4**. Make 32 **Unit 4's**.

Fig. 2 **Unit 4** (make 32)

6. Place 1 **small square** and 1 **square** right sides together and matching edges. Sew diagonally across **small square** (**Fig. 3a**). Trim 1/4" beyond stitching (**Fig. 3b**) and press open to make **Unit 5**. Make 32 **Unit 5's**.

Fig. 3a **Fig. 3b**

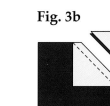

Unit 5 (make 32)

7. Place 1 **Unit 5** and 1 **Unit 4** right sides together and matching edges. Sew diagonally across **Unit 5** (**Fig. 4a**). Trim 1/4" beyond stitching (**Fig. 4b**) and press open to make **Unit 6**. Make 32 **Unit 6's**.

Fig. 4a **Fig. 4b**

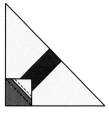

Unit 6 (make 32)

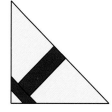

8. Sew 1 **Unit 3** and 1 **Unit 6** together to make **Unit 7**. Make 32 **Unit 7's**.

Unit 7 (make 32)

9. Sew **short**, then **long inner borders** to **Unit 7** to complete **Block**. Make 32 **Blocks**.

Block (make 32)

10. Referring to **Assembly Diagram**, page 14, sew **corner setting triangles**, **sashing triangles**, **sashing strips**, **setting triangles**, **sashing squares**, and **Blocks** together into **Rows**. Sew **Rows** together to complete **Quilt Top**.

COMPLETING THE QUILT

1. Follow **Quilting**, page 151, to mark, layer, and quilt using **Quilting Diagram**, page 15, as a suggestion. Our quilt is hand quilted.
2. Cut a 30" square of binding fabric. Follow **Binding**, page 155, to bind quilt using 2 1/2"w bias binding with mitered corners.

13

TREE OF LIFE PILLOW

PILLOW SIZE: 15" x 15"

YARDAGE REQUIREMENTS

Yardage is based on 45"w fabric.

■ ³/8 yd of red solid

□ ³/8 yd of cream print

■ ¹/8 yd of green print
   ¹/2 yd for pillow top backing
   ¹/2 yd for pillow back
   17" x 17" batting

You will also need:
   polyester fiberfill

CUTTING OUT THE PIECES
All measurements include a ¹/4" seam allowance. Follow
***Rotary Cutting**, page 144, to cut fabric.*

1. **From red solid:** ■
    * Cut 1 **large square** 8" x 8" for triangle-squares.
    * Cut 1 square 6³/8" x 6³/8". Cut square once diagonally to make 2 **triangles** (you will need 1 and have 1 left over).
    * Cut 4 **corner squares** 3¹/2" x 3¹/2".
    * Cut 1 **short inner border** 1¹/2" x 8³/4".
    * Cut 1 **long inner border** 1¹/2" x 9³/4".
    * Cut 1 **trunk** 1¹/2" x 4¹/2".
    * Cut 1 **square** 2" x 2".

2. From cream print:
- Cut 1 **large square** 8" x 8" for triangle-squares.
- Cut 2 **squares** $1\frac{7}{8}$" x $1\frac{7}{8}$".
- Cut 1 square 6" x 6". Cut square twice diagonally to make 2 **triangles** (you will need 2 and have 2 left over).
- Cut 1 **small square** $1\frac{1}{4}$" x $1\frac{1}{4}$".

3. From green print: ▣
- Cut 4 **outer borders** $3\frac{1}{2}$" x $9\frac{3}{4}$".

ASSEMBLING THE PILLOW TOP

Follow Piecing and Pressing, page 146, to make pillow top.

1. To make triangle-squares, place red and cream **large squares** right sides together. Referring to **Fig. 1**, follow **Making Triangle-Squares**, page 147, to complete 18 **triangle-squares**.

Fig. 1   triangle-square (make 18)

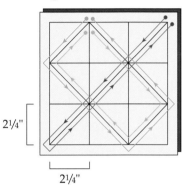

2. Follow Steps 2 - 9 of **Assembling the Quilt Top**, page 12, to make 1 **Block**.
3. Sew 1 **outer border** each to top and bottom of **Block**. Sew 1 **corner square** to each end of remaining **outer borders**; sew **outer borders** to sides of **Block** to complete **Pillow Top**.

COMPLETING THE PILLOW

1. Follow **Quilting**, page 151, to mark, layer, and quilt using **Quilting Diagram** as a suggestion. Our pillow top is hand quilted.
2. Follow **Making the Pillow**, page 158, to complete pillow.

Pillow Top Diagram

Quilting Diagram

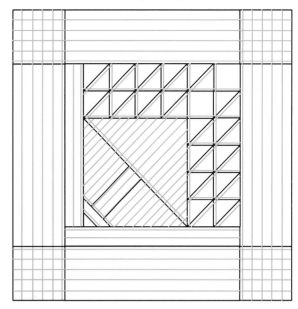

DELECTABLE MOUNTAINS DOLL QUILT

SKILL LEVEL: 1 2 3 4 5
BLOCK SIZE: $6\frac{1}{4}$" x $6\frac{1}{4}$"
QUILT SIZE: 25" x 32"

YARDAGE REQUIREMENTS

Yardage is based on 45"w fabric.

☐ $1\frac{1}{8}$ yds of cream solid
■ 1 yd of red solid
$\frac{7}{8}$ yd for backing
$\frac{1}{4}$ yd for binding
29" x 35" batting

CUTTING OUT THE PIECES

All measurements include a $\frac{1}{4}$" seam allowance. Follow Rotary Cutting, page 144, to cut fabric.

1. **From cream solid:** ☐
- Cut 2 strips $7\frac{1}{2}$"w. From these strips, cut 10 squares $7\frac{1}{2}$" x $7\frac{1}{2}$". Cut squares twice diagonally to make 40 **triangles**.
- Cut 2 strips $1\frac{3}{8}$"w. From these strips, cut 40 **squares** $1\frac{3}{8}$" x $1\frac{3}{8}$".
- Cut 2 **rectangles** 12" x 19" for triangle-squares.

2. **From red solid:** ■
- Cut 2 strips 5"w. From these strips, cut 10 squares 5" x 5". Cut squares twice diagonally to make 40 **medium triangles**.
- Cut 2 strips $1\frac{3}{4}$"w. From these strips, cut 40 squares $1\frac{3}{4}$" x $1\frac{3}{4}$". Cut squares once diagonally to make 80 **small triangles**.
- Cut 2 **rectangles** 12" x 19" for triangle-squares.

15

ASSEMBLING THE QUILT TOP

*Follow **Piecing and Pressing**, page 146, to make quilt top.*

1. To make triangle-squares, place 1 cream and 1 red **rectangle** right sides together. Referring to **Fig. 1**, follow **Making Triangle-Squares**, page 147, to complete 120 **triangle-squares**. Repeat with remaining rectangles to make a total of 240 **triangle-squares**.

Fig. 1

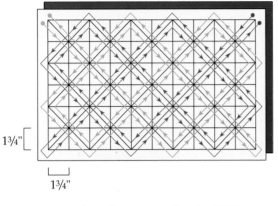

triangle-square (make 240)

2. Sew 3 **triangle-squares** and 1 **small triangle** together to make **Unit 1**. Make 40 **Unit 1's**. Sew 1 **square**, 3 **triangle-squares**, and 1 **small triangle** together to make **Unit 2**. Make 40 **Unit 2's**.

Unit 1 (make 40)

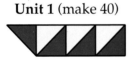

Unit 2 (make 40)

3. Sew 1 **Unit 1**, 1 **medium triangle**, and 1 **Unit 2** together to make **Unit 3**. Make 40 **Unit 3's**.

Unit 3 (make 40)

4. Sew 2 **Unit 3's** and 2 **triangles** together to make **Block**. Make 20 **Blocks**.

Block (make 20)

5. Sew 4 **Blocks** together to make **Row**. Make 5 **Rows**.

Row (make 5)

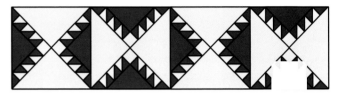

6. Referring to **Quilt Top Diagram**, sew **Rows** together to complete **Quilt Top**.

COMPLETING THE QUILT

1. Follow **Quilting**, page 151, to mark, layer, and quilt using **Quilting Diagram** as a suggestion. Our quilt is hand quilted.
2. Follow **Binding**, page 155, to bind quilt using 1¾"w straight-grain binding with mitered corners.

Quilt Top Diagram

Quilting Diagram

KANSAS TROUBLES PILLOW

BLOCK SIZE: 4³/₈" x 4³/₈"
PILLOW SIZE: 14" x 14" (including ruffle)

YARDAGE REQUIREMENTS

Yardage is based on 45"w fabric.

☐ ⁵/₈ yd of cream print
■ ¹/₄ yd of red solid
▨ ¹/₈ yd of green print
13" x 13" batting
³/₈ yd for pillow top backing
³/₈ yd for pillow back
1¹/₄ yds of 1³/₄"w bias strip for welting
1¹/₄ yds of ³/₁₆" cord for welting

You will also need:
polyester fiberfill

CUTTING OUT THE PIECES

All measurements include a ¹/₄" seam allowance. Follow Rotary Cutting, page 144, to cut fabric.

1. **From cream print:** ☐
   - Cut 1 **rectangle** 7" x 9" for triangle-squares.
   - Cut 2 squares 5¹/₄" x 5¹/₄". Cut squares once diagonally to make 4 **large triangles**.
   - Cut 4 **squares** 1³/₈" x 1³/₈".

2. **From red solid:** ■
   - Cut 1 **rectangle** 7" x 9" for triangle-squares.
   - Cut 2 squares 3¹/₂" x 3¹/₂". Cut squares once diagonally to make 4 **medium triangles**.
   - Cut 4 squares 1³/₄" x 1³/₄". Cut squares once diagonally to make 8 **small triangles**.

ASSEMBLING THE PILLOW TOP

Follow Piecing and Pressing, page 146, to make pillow top.

1. To make triangle-squares, place cream and red **rectangles** right sides together. Referring to

Fig. 1, follow **Making Triangle-Squares**, page 147, to complete 24 **triangle-squares**.

Fig. 1

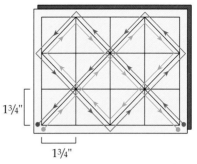

1³/₄"

1³/₄"

triangle-square (make 24)

2. Follow Steps 2 and 3 of **Assembling the Quilt Top**, page 12, to make 4 **Unit 3's** (you will need 4 **Unit 1's** and 4 **Unit 2's**).

3. Sew 1 **Unit 3** and 1 **large triangle** together to make **Block**. Make 4 **Blocks**.

Block (make 4)

4. Referring to photo, sew **Blocks** together to complete **Pillow Top**.

COMPLETING THE PILLOW

1. Follow **Quilting**, page 151, to mark, layer, and quilt using **Quilting Diagram**, this page, as a suggestion. Our pillow top is hand quilted.

2. Follow **Adding Welting to Pillow Top**, page 158, to add welting.

3. For ruffle, cut 1 **strip** 3" x 91" from cream print and 1 **ruffle trim** 1¹/₄" x 91" from green print, piecing as necessary. Matching long raw edges, sew right side of **ruffle trim** to wrong side of **strip**. Press 1 long edge of ruffle trim ¹/₄" to wrong side. Fold pressed edge over to right side of strip, covering stitching line; topstitch in place. Sew short edges of ruffle together to form a large circle. Follow Steps 3 - 5 of **Adding Ruffle to Pillow Top**, page 158, to attach ruffle.

4. Follow **Making the Pillow**, page 158, to complete pillow.

STAR OF BETHLEHEM COLLECTION

As resplendent as the brilliant star that led the three Magi to a humble stable, our Star of Bethlehem quilt will be an enlightening touch to your decor. The spectrum of warm hues in the star medallion is created with rows of diamond pieces — all easily cut from strip-pieced sets. Complementing the angular shape of the "rays," the sawtooth borders are pieced with simple triangle-squares. For length, we added rows of basic Nine-Patch blocks for the pillow flip and bottom edge of the quilt. The deep outer border and open areas within the quilt are ideal for letting masterpiece quilting shine!

A *smaller version of our Star of Bethlehem quilt, this wall hanging (below) is rich with royal beauty. Simple strip-set units are pieced together for the radiant star and inner border, and a striped floral fabric for the outer border produces the look of many intricate borders in one easy step. We also borrowed motifs from our quilt to create coordinating throw pillows (opposite). Accented with a star medallion or a sawtooth border, they make charming accessories.*

STAR OF BETHLEHEM QUILT

SKILL LEVEL: 1 2 3 4 5
QUILT SIZE: 102" x 119"

YARDAGE REQUIREMENTS

Yardage is based on 45"w fabric.

- 5 yds of cream print for background
- 3¼ yds of red print for outer borders
- 1⅜ yds of burgundy print for triangle-squares
- ⅝ yd *each* of red print, gold print, burgundy print, tan print, green print, blue print, and navy print for star
- ⅜ yd of navy print for outer border corners
  9 yds for backing
  1 yd for binding
  120" x 120" batting

CUTTING OUT THE PIECES

All measurements include a ¼" seam allowance. Follow **Rotary Cutting***, page 144, to cut fabric.*

1. **From cream print:**
   - Cut 4 **corner squares** 23" x 23".
   - Cut 1 square 33" x 33". Cut square twice diagonally to make 4 **side triangles**.
   - Cut 8 squares 9¾" x 9¾". Cut squares twice diagonally to make 32 **large border triangles**.
   - Cut 4 **small rectangles** 3¼" x 9".
   - Cut 4 squares 5⅛" x 5⅛". Cut squares once diagonally to make 8 **small border triangles**.
   - Cut 2 lengthwise **top/bottom narrow borders** 2½" x 78½".
   - Cut 2 lengthwise **side narrow borders** 2½" x 74½".
   - Cut 4 **rectangles** 19" x 22" for triangle-squares.

2. **From red print for outer borders:**
   - Cut 2 lengthwise **side outer borders** 10" x 99½".
   - Cut 2 lengthwise **top/bottom outer borders** 10" x 82½".
   - Cut 2 squares 10⅜" x 10⅜". Cut squares once diagonally to make 4 **outer border corner triangles**.

3. **From burgundy print for triangle-squares:**
   - Cut 4 **rectangles** 19" x 22" for triangle-squares.

4. **From red print, gold print, burgundy print, tan print, green print, blue print, and navy print:**
   - Cut 7 **strips** 2½"w from *each* fabric. From 1 end of *each* strip, cut 4 **squares** 2½" x 2½".

5. **From navy print for outer border corners:**
   - Cut 2 squares 10⅜" x 10⅜". Cut squares once diagonally to make 4 **outer border corner triangles**.

ASSEMBLING THE QUILT TOP

Follow **Piecing and Pressing***, page 146, to make quilt top.*

1. Sew **strips** together in the color order shown, adding each new strip 2" from the end of the previous strip, to make **Strip Sets A, B, C, D, E, F,** and **G**.

Strip Set A (make 1)

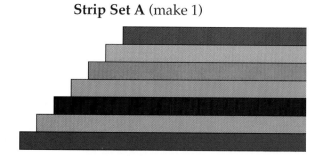

Strip Set B (make 1)

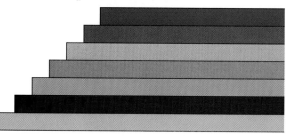

Strip Set C (make 1)

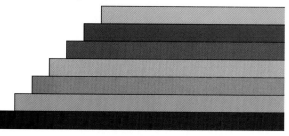

Strip Set D (make 1)

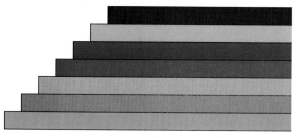

Strip Set E (make 1)

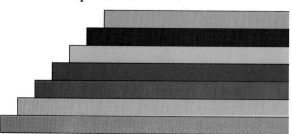

Strip Set F (make 1)

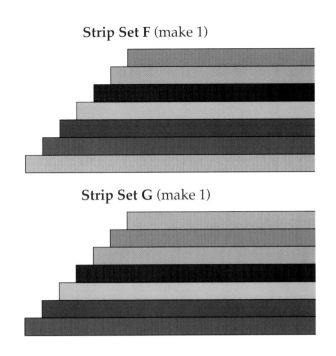

Strip Set G (make 1)

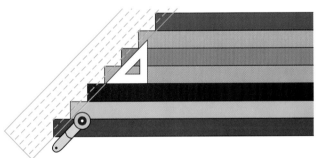

2. Referring to **Fig. 1**, use a large right-angle triangle aligned with a seam to determine an accurate 45° cutting line. Use rotary cutter and rotary cutting ruler to trim the uneven ends from 1 end of each **Strip Set**.

Fig. 1

3. Aligning the 45° mark on the rotary cutting ruler (shown in pink) with a seam and aligning the 2½" mark with the cut edge made in Step 2, cut across **Strip Sets** at 2½" intervals as shown in **Fig. 2**.

Fig. 2

2½"

From **Strip Set A**, cut 8 **Unit 1's**.

Unit 1 (cut 8)

From **Strip Set B**, cut 8 **Unit 2's**.

Unit 2 (cut 8)

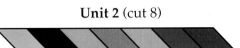

From **Strip Set C**, cut 8 **Unit 3's**.

Unit 3 (cut 8)

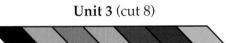

From **Strip Set D**, cut 8 **Unit 4's**.

Unit 4 (cut 8)

From **Strip Set E**, cut 8 **Unit 5's**.

Unit 5 (cut 8)

From **Strip Set F**, cut 8 **Unit 6's**.

Unit 6 (cut 8)

From **Strip Set G**, cut 8 **Unit 7's**.

Unit 7 (cut 8)

4. When making Unit 8's, refer to **Fig. 3** to match long edges of units. Seams will cross ¼" from cut edges of fabric. Pin and stitch as shown in **Fig. 3**. Sew 1 **Unit 1**, 1 **Unit 2**, 1 **Unit 3**, 1 **Unit 4**, 1 **Unit 5**, 1 **Unit 6**, and 1 **Unit 7** together in order shown, page 24, to make **Unit 8**. Make 8 **Unit 8's**.

Fig. 3

Unit 8 (make 8)

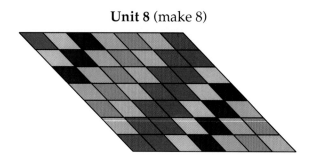

5. To make Unit 9, place 2 **Unit 8's** right sides together, carefully matching edges and seams; pin. Stitch in direction shown in **Fig. 4**, ending stitching 1/4" from edge of fabric (you may find it helpful to mark a small dot at this point before sewing) and backstitching at end of seam. Make 4 **Unit 9's**.

Fig. 4

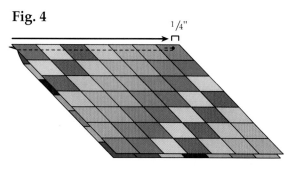

Unit 9 (make 4)

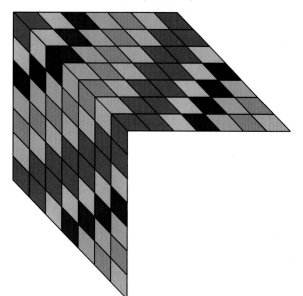

6. Referring to **Quilt Top Diagram**, page 26, sew **Unit 9's** together to make **Star**, ending stitching 1/4" from edges and backstitching each seam.
7. Follow Steps 2 and 3 of **Working With Diamond Shapes**, page 148, to attach **side triangles**, then **corner squares** to **Star** to make center section of quilt top. (Side triangles and corner squares are cut larger than finished measurement in order to "float" the star. Match dots at inside corners and pin, then match and pin remainder of seam before stitching.)

8. Carefully trim center section to measure 70 1/2" x 70 1/2".
9. To make triangle-squares, place 1 burgundy and 1 cream **rectangle** right sides together. Referring to **Fig. 5**, follow **Making Triangle-Squares**, page 147, to complete 84 **triangle-squares**. Repeat with remaining **rectangles** to make a total of 336 **triangle-squares** (you will need 304 and have 32 left over).

Fig. 5

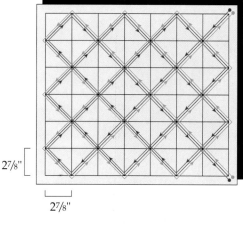

triangle-square (make 336)

10. (*Note:* For Steps 10 - 17, refer to **Quilt Top Diagram**, page 26.) Sew 35 **triangle-squares** together to make **Side Inner Sawtooth Border**. Make 2 **Side Inner Sawtooth Borders**.
11. Sew 37 **triangle-squares** together to make **Top/Bottom Inner Sawtooth Border**. Make 2 **Top/Bottom Inner Sawtooth Borders**.
12. Sew **Side**, then **Top** and **Bottom Inner Sawtooth Borders** to center section of quilt top.
13. Sew **side**, then **top** and **bottom narrow borders** to center section of quilt top.
14. Sew 39 **triangle-squares** together to make **Side Outer Sawtooth Border**. Make 2 **Side Outer Sawtooth Borders**.
15. Sew 41 **triangle-squares** together to make **Top/Bottom Outer Sawtooth Borders**. Make 2 **Top/Bottom Outer Sawtooth Borders**.
16. Sew **Side**, then **Top** and **Bottom Outer Sawtooth Borders** to center section of quilt top.
17. To make nine-patch blocks, sew **squares** together in random color combinations, using 5 squares of 1 fabric and 4 of another for each block. Make 18 **Nine-Patch Blocks** (you will have some squares left over).

Nine-Patch Block (make 18)

18. Sew 1 **large border triangle**, 1 **Nine-Patch Block**, 2 **small border triangles**, and 1 **small rectangle** together to make **Unit 10**. Make 4 **Unit 10's**.

Unit 10 (make 4)

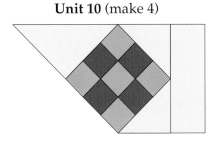

19. Sew 1 **Nine-Patch Block** and 2 **large border triangles** together to make **Unit 11**. Make 14 **Unit 11's**.

Unit 11 (make 14)

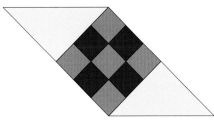

20. Referring to **Quilt Top Diagram**, sew 2 **Unit 10's** and 7 **Unit 11's** together to make **Nine-Patch Border**. Make 2 **Nine-Patch Borders**.

21. Sew **Nine-Patch Borders** to top and bottom edges of center section of quilt top.

22. Sew 1 red print and 1 navy print **outer border corner triangle** together to make **Outer Border Corner Square**. Make 4 **Outer Border Corner Squares**.

23. Sew 1 **Outer Border Corner Square** to each end of each **top/bottom outer border**. Sew **side**, then **top** and **bottom outer borders** to center section to complete **Quilt Top**.

COMPLETING THE QUILT

1. Follow **Quilting**, page 151, to mark, layer, and quilt using **Quilting Diagram** as a suggestion. Our quilt is hand quilted.

2. Cut a 34" square of binding fabric. Follow **Binding**, page 155, to bind quilt using 2¹/₂"w bias binding with mitered corners.

Quilting Diagram

STAR OF BETHLEHEM WALL HANGING

SKILL LEVEL: 1 2 3 4 5
WALL HANGING SIZE: 42" x 42"

YARDAGE REQUIREMENTS

Yardage is based on 45"w fabric.

- 1³/₈ yds of floral stripe
- ³/₄ yd of cream solid
- ¹/₂ yd of burgundy print
- ¹/₂ yd of tan print
- ³/₈ yd *each* of blue print and navy print
  2¹/₂ yds for backing and hanging sleeve
  ³/₄ yd for binding
  46" x 46" batting

CUTTING OUT THE PIECES

All measurements include a ¹/₄" seam allowance. Follow **Rotary Cutting***, page 144, to cut fabric.*

1. **From floral stripe:**
   - Cut 4 lengthwise **outer borders** 5" x 45".

2. **From cream solid:**
   - Cut 4 **corner squares** 9" x 9".
   - Cut 1 square 13¹/₄" x 13¹/₄". Cut square twice diagonally to make 4 **side triangles**.

3. **From burgundy print:**
   - Cut 5 **strips** 2"w.
   - Cut 1 **strip** 6"w.

4. **From tan print:**
   - Cut 6 **strips** 2"w.

5. **From blue print and navy print:**
   - Cut 5 **strips** 2"w from *each* fabric.

ASSEMBLING THE WALL HANGING TOP

Follow **Piecing and Pressing***, page 146, to make wall hanging top.*

1. Sew **strips** together in the color order shown, adding each new strip 1¹/₂" from the end of the previous strip, to make **Strip Sets A**, **B**, **C**, **D**, and **E**. Make 1 **Strip Set A**, 2 **Strip Set B's**, and 1 each of **Strip Sets C**, **D**, and **E**.

2. Follow Step 2 of **Assembling the Quilt Top**, page 23, to trim the uneven ends of **Strip Sets** at a 45° angle.

3. Aligning the 45° mark on the rotary cutting ruler with a seam and aligning the 2" mark with the cut edge made in Step 2, cut across strip sets at 2" intervals (see **Fig. 2**, page 23) to cut indicated numbers of units from each strip set.

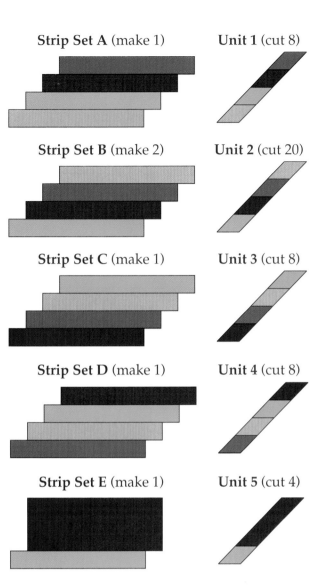

Strip Set A (make 1) — Unit 1 (cut 8)
Strip Set B (make 2) — Unit 2 (cut 20)
Strip Set C (make 1) — Unit 3 (cut 8)
Strip Set D (make 1) — Unit 4 (cut 8)
Strip Set E (make 1) — Unit 5 (cut 4)

4. When making Unit 6's, refer to **Fig. 3**, page 23, to match long edges of units. Seams will cross ¹/₄" from cut edges of fabric. Sew 1 **Unit 1**, 1 **Unit 2**, 1 **Unit 3**, and 1 **Unit 4** together to make **Unit 6**. Make 8 **Unit 6's**.

Unit 6 (make 8)

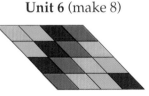

5. Use **Unit 6's**, **squares**, and **triangles** and follow Steps 5 and 6 of **Assembling the Quilt Top**, page 24, and Steps 2 and 3 of **Working With Diamond Shapes**, page 148, to make center section of wall hanging.

6. Sew 3 **Unit 2's** and 1 **Unit 5** together to make **Pieced Border Unit**. Make 4 **Pieced Border Units**.

Pieced Border Unit (make 4)

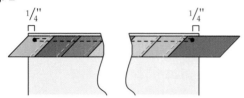

7. Referring to **Fig. 1**, sew 1 **Pieced Border Unit** to 1 edge of center section of wall hanging top, beginning and ending stitching exactly ¼" from each corner of center section and backstitching at beginning and end of seam. Do not trim off excess portion of **Unit 5** at this time. Repeat for remaining edges.

Fig. 1

8. Fold 1 corner of center section diagonally with right sides together, matching outer edges of borders (**Fig. 2**). Beginning at point where previous

seams ended, stitch to outer corner. Trim off excess **Pieced Border Unit**. Repeat for remaining corners.

Fig. 2

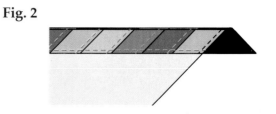

9. Referring to **Wall Hanging Top Diagram**, follow **Adding Mitered Borders**, page 151, to add **outer borders** to complete **Wall Hanging Top**.

COMPLETING THE WALL HANGING

1. Follow **Quilting**, page 151, to mark, layer, and quilt using **Quilting Diagram** as a suggestion. Our wall hanging is hand quilted.
2. Follow **Making a Hanging Sleeve**, page 157, to attach hanging sleeve to wall hanging back.
3. Cut a 22" square of binding fabric. Follow **Binding**, page 155, to bind wall hanging using 2½"w bias binding with mitered corners.

Quilting Diagram

STAR OF BETHLEHEM PILLOW

PILLOW SIZE: 22" x 22"

YARDAGE REQUIREMENTS

Yardage is based on 45"w fabric.

■ ½ yd of rust print

☐ ⅜ yd of cream print

▨ ⅛ yd *each* of gold print, blue print, and navy print
   26" x 26" pillow top backing
   ¾ yd for pillow back
   26" x 26" batting

You will also need:
   polyester fiberfill

CUTTING OUT THE PIECES

All measurements include a ¹/₄" seam allowance. Follow Rotary Cutting, page 144, to cut fabric.

1. **From rust print:** ■
    - Cut 4 **border strips** 2¹/₄"w.
    - Cut 3 **strips** 1³/₄"w.

2. **From cream print:** ☐
    - Cut 4 **corner squares** 5³/₄" x 5³/₄".
    - Cut 1 square 8³/₄" x 8³/₄". Cut square twice diagonally to make 4 **side triangles**.

3. **From gold print, blue print, and navy print:** ▨
    - Cut 2 **strips** 1³/₄"w from *each* fabric.

MAKING THE PILLOW

Follow Piecing and Pressing, page 146, to make pillow.

1. Sew **strips** together in color order shown in Step 3, page 30, adding each new strip 1¹/₄" from the end of the previous strip, to make **Strip Sets A**, **B**, and **C**.

2. Follow Step 2 of **Assembling the Quilt Top**, page 23, to trim uneven ends of **Strip Sets** at a 45° angle.

3. Aligning the 45° mark on the rotary cutting ruler with a seam and aligning the 1³/₄" mark with the cut edge made in Step 2, cut across strip sets at 1³/₄" intervals (refer to **Fig. 2**, page 23) to cut 8 **Units** from each **Strip Set**.

Strip Set A (make 1)   **Unit 1** (cut 8)

Strip Set B (make 1)   **Unit 2** (cut 8)

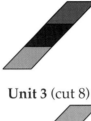

Strip Set C (make 1)   **Unit 3** (cut 8)

4. When making Unit 4's, refer to **Fig. 3**, page 23, to match long edges of units. Seams will cross ¹/₄" from cut edges of fabric. Sew 1 **Unit 1**, 1 **Unit 2**, and 1 **Unit 3** together to make **Unit 4**. Make 8 **Unit 4's**.

Unit 4 (make 8)

5. Use **Unit 4's**, **squares**, and **triangles** and follow Steps 5 and 6 of **Assembling the Quilt Top**, page 24, and Steps 2 and 3 of **Working With Diamond Shapes**, page 148, to make center section of pillow top.

6. Sew **border strips** to opposite edges of center section, trimming off remainder of **border strips** after stitching. Repeat with remaining edges to complete **Pillow Top**.

7. Follow **Quilting**, page 151, to mark, layer, and quilt. Our pillow top is hand quilted.

8. Follow **Making the Pillow**, page 158, to complete pillow.

Pillow Top Diagram

SAWTOOTH PILLOW

PILLOW SIZE: 18" x 18"

YARDAGE REQUIREMENTS
Yardage is based on 45"w fabric.

☐ ³/₈ yd of cream print
■ ³/₈ yd of rust print
■ ¹/₄ yd of dark rust print
▣ ¹/₈ yd of gold print
22" x 22" pillow top backing
⁵/₈ yd for pillow back
2¹/₄ yds of 2¹/₂"w bias strip for welting
2¹/₄ yds of ¹/₄" cord for welting

You will also need:
polyester fiberfill

CUTTING OUT THE PIECES
All measurements include a ¹/₄" seam allowance. Follow
Rotary Cutting, *page 144, to cut fabric.*

1. **From cream print:** ☐
   - Cut 1 **square** 8¹/₂" x 8¹/₂".
   - Cut 1 **large rectangle** 7" x 16" for triangle-square A's.
   - Cut 1 **small rectangle** 4" x 7" for triangle-square B's.

2. **From rust print:** ■
   - Cut 4 **outer borders** 2¹/₂" x 13¹/₂".
   - Cut 1 **small rectangle** 4" x 7" for triangle-square B's.

3. **From dark rust print:** ■
   - Cut 1 **large rectangle** 7" x 16" for triangle-square A's.

4. **From gold print:** ▣
   - Cut 2 **top/bottom inner borders** 1" x 12¹/₂".
   - Cut 2 **side inner borders** 1" x 13¹/₂".

MAKING THE PILLOW

*Follow **Piecing and Pressing**, page 146, to make pillow top.*

1. To make triangle-square A's, place **large rectangles** right sides together. Referring to **Fig. 1**, follow **Making Triangle-Squares**, page 147, to make 20 **triangle-square A's**.

Fig. 1

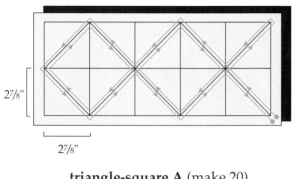

triangle-square A (make 20)

2. Sew 4 **triangle-square A's** together to make 1 **Top Sawtooth Border**. Sew 4 **triangle-square A's** together to make 1 **Bottom Sawtooth Border**.

Top Sawtooth Border (make 1)

Bottom Sawtooth Border (make 1)

3. Sew 6 **triangle-square A's** together to make 1 **Left Sawtooth Border**. Sew 6 **triangle-square A's** together to make 1 **Right Sawtooth Border**.

Left Sawtooth Border (make 1)

Right Sawtooth Border (make 1)

4. Sew **Top** and **Bottom**, then **Left** and **Right Sawtooth Borders** to **square** to make center section of pillow top.
5. Sew **top**, **bottom**, then **side inner borders** to center section.
6. To make triangle-square B's, place **small rectangles** right sides together. Referring to **Fig. 2**, follow **Making Triangle-Squares**, page 147, to make 4 **triangle-square B's**.

Fig. 2

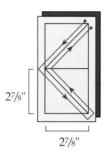

triangle-square B (make 4)

7. Sew **outer borders** to top and bottom edges of center section. Sew 1 **triangle-square B** to each end of remaining **outer borders**; sew **borders** to side edges of center section to complete **Pillow Top**.
8. Follow **Quilting**, page 151, to mark, layer, and quilt. Our pillow top is hand quilted (see photo).
9. Follow **Pillow Finishing**, page 158, to complete pillow with welting.

Pillow Top Diagram

SQUARE DANCE

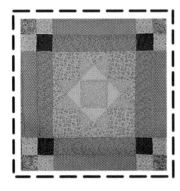

Much of the excitement created during a pioneer quilting bee was in anticipation of the evening's rousing square dance. Husbands and beaus would don their Sunday best, join the stitchers for a grand supper, and then whirl the night away to the fiddle's call of "Wabash Cannonball" or perhaps even "Turkey in the Straw." Resembling a promenade of dancing calicoes, our Square Dance quilt is pieced using a kaleidoscope of charming prints. Each Ohio Star block is surrounded by a double border and matching sashing strips that create a classic patchwork look. The basic elements of the quilt are easy to assemble using handy strip-piecing and rotary cutting shortcuts.

SQUARE DANCE QUILT

SKILL LEVEL: 1 2 3 4 5
BLOCK SIZE: 22" x 22"
QUILT SIZE: 97" x 112"

Making this quilt top is a great way to use scraps left over from other projects. Although you can cut pieces for this scrap quilt using rotary cutting techniques, it is easier to piece using the more traditional block-at-a-time approach.

YARDAGE REQUIREMENTS

Yardage is based on 45"w fabric.

- 12 - 15 yds of assorted scraps
  8³/₄ yds for backing
  1¹/₄ yds for binding
  120" x 120" batting

CUTTING OUT THE PIECES

All measurements include a ¹/₄" seam allowance.
*Follow **Rotary Cutting**, page 144, to cut fabric for blocks and sashing.*

FOR BLOCKS

1. Study the **Fabric Placement Diagram**, page 36. Each letter in the diagram represents placement for 1 fabric. Choose 8 different scrap fabrics for 1 block and label them A - H.
2. Cut pieces from fabrics as indicated below.
   From Fabric A:
   - Cut 4 **square A's** 4¹/₂" x 4¹/₂".
   - Cut 1 square 5¹/₄" x 5¹/₄". Cut square twice diagonally to make 4 **triangle A's**.
   From Fabric B:
   - Cut 1 square 5¹/₄" x 5¹/₄". Cut square twice diagonally to make 4 **triangle B's**.
   From Fabric C:
   - Cut 1 **square C** 4¹/₂" x 4¹/₂".
   - Cut 2 squares 5¹/₄" x 5¹/₄". Cut squares twice diagonally to make 8 **triangle C's**.
   From Fabric D:
   - Cut 4 **strip D's** 3" x 12¹/₂".
   From Fabric E:
   - Cut 4 **strip E's** 3" x 12¹/₂".
   From Fabric F:
   - Cut 8 **corner square F's** 3" x 3".
   From Fabric G:
   - Cut 4 **corner square G's** 3" x 3".
   From Fabric H:
   - Cut 4 **corner square H's** 3" x 3".
3. Label all pieces for block and group into separate stacks.
4. Repeat Steps 1 - 3 to cut fabric pieces for each of 16 blocks in assorted color combinations, using photo as a suggestion. Keep in mind that each fabric may be repeated in another area of a different block — Fabric A in 1 block may be used as Fabric H in another block.

FOR SASHING

1. **From assorted scraps:**
   - Cut 48 **sashing strips** 3" x 12¹/₂".
   - Cut 219 **sashing squares** 3" x 3" (you will need 96 sets of 2 matching squares and 27 unmatched squares).

ASSEMBLING THE QUILT TOP

*Follow **Piecing and Pressing**, page 146, to make quilt top.*

1. Sew 1 **triangle A**, 1 **triangle B**, and 2 **triangle C's** together to make **Unit 1**. Make 4 **Unit 1's**.

Unit 1 (make 4)

2. Sew 2 **square A's** and 1 **Unit 1** together to make **Unit 2**. Make 2 **Unit 2's**.

Unit 2 (make 2)

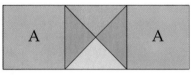

3. Sew 2 **Unit 1's** and 1 **square C** together to make 1 **Unit 3**.

Unit 3 (make 1)

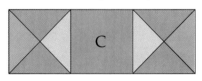

4. Sew **Unit 2's** and **Unit 3** together to make 1 **Unit 4**.

Unit 4 (make 1)

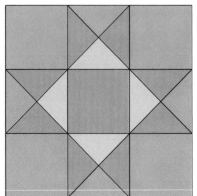

5. Sew 1 **strip D** and 1 **strip E** together to make **Unit 5**. Make 4 **Unit 5's**.

Unit 5 (make 4)

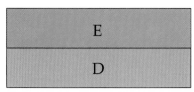

6. Sew 2 **Unit 5's** and **Unit 4** together to make 1 **Unit 6**.

Unit 6 (make 1)

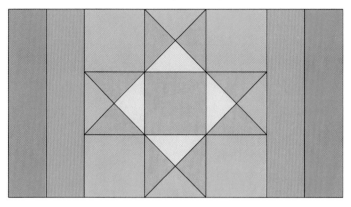

7. Sew 2 **corner square F's**, 1 **corner square G**, and 1 **corner square H** together to make **Unit 7**. Make 4 **Unit 7's**.

Unit 7 (make 4)

8. Sew 2 **Unit 7's** and 1 **Unit 5** together to make **Unit 8**. Make 2 **Unit 8's**.

Unit 8 (make 2)

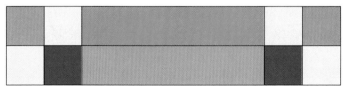

9. Sew **Unit 8's** to top and bottom of **Unit 6** to make **Block**.

Block

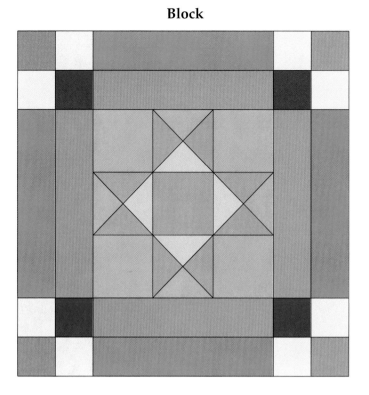

10. Repeat Steps 1 - 9 to make 16 **Blocks**.
11. Sew 2 sets of matching **sashing squares** and 1 **sashing strip** together to make **Sashing Unit**. Make 48 **Sashing Units**.

Sashing Unit (make 48)

12. Sew 4 **Blocks** and 3 **Sashing Units** together to make **Row**. Make 4 **Rows**.

Row (make 4)

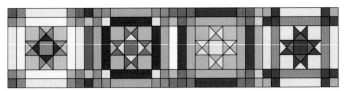

13. Sew 4 **Sashing Units** and 3 **sashing squares** together to make **Sashing Row**. Make 9 **Sashing Rows**.

Sashing Row (make 9)

14. Sew 3 **Sashing Rows** together to make **Sashing Border**. Make 2 **Sashing Borders**.

Sashing Border (make 2)

15. Referring to **Quilt Top Diagram**, sew **Sashing Borders**, **Rows**, and **Sashing Rows** together to complete **Quilt Top**.

COMPLETING THE QUILT
1. Follow **Quilting**, page 151, to mark, layer, and quilt. Our quilt is hand quilted in the ditch along all seamlines.
2. Cut a 34" square of binding fabric. Follow **Binding**, page 155, to bind quilt using 2¹/₂"w bias binding with mitered corners.

Fabric Placement Diagram

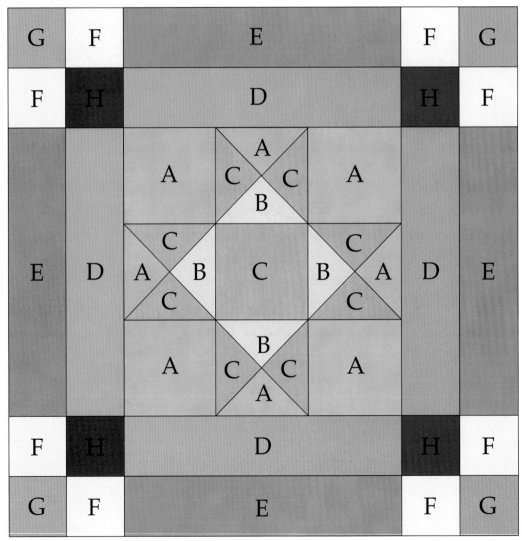

Each letter in the diagram represents placement for 1 fabric.

FOUR SEASONS COLLECTION

For prairie settlers, each season was a unique chapter in the quilt-making process. Winter snows kept stitchers indoors where they diligently pieced an assortment of quilt blocks. With the spring thaw, distant neighbors gathered to assemble the tops during bustling quilting bees. Quilts were stored away in the heat of summer, but harvesttime brought abundant wool and cotton for weaving the homey cloth that would become the next season's patchwork projects. Featuring the rich hues enjoyed throughout the year, our Four Seasons quilt has a latticework look created with two basic blocks — the classic Nine Patch and the Snowball. The quilt is simple to make using fast strip piecing and a quick technique for creating accurate triangle corners.

Display your love of quilting throughout the changing seasons with this charming accent (opposite). A smaller version of our quilt, the wall hanging features seasonal tree and leaf motifs machine appliquéd over Nine-Patch and Snowball blocks. Pieced with diamond-look units, the border is created using simple triangles and squares set on point. Designs from our wall hanging can also dress up a purchased sweater vest or chambray shirt (below). For an easy finish, we simply fused the appliqués in place and edged them with machine satin stitching.

FOUR SEASONS QUILT

SKILL LEVEL: 1 2 3 4 5
BLOCK SIZE: 7½" x 7½"
QUILT SIZE: 84" x 99"

YARDAGE REQUIREMENTS

Yardage is based on 45"w fabric.

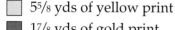

- 5⅝ yds of yellow print
- 1⅞ yds of gold print
- 1⅝ yds of green print
- 1⅝ yds of blue print
- 1⅝ yds of rust print
  7¾ yds for backing
  1 yd for binding
  90" x 108" batting

CUTTING OUT THE PIECES

All measurements include a ¼" seam allowance. Follow Rotary Cutting, page 144, to cut fabric.

1. **From yellow print:**
   - Cut 10 strips 8"w. From these strips, cut 49 **large squares** 8" x 8".
   - Cut 21 **strips** 3"w.
   - Cut 6 strips 6¼"w. From these strips, cut 31 squares 6¼" x 6¼". Cut squares twice diagonally to make 124 **border triangles**.
   - Cut 2 squares 5⅞" x 5⅞". Cut squares once diagonally to make 4 **corner unit triangles**.

2. **From gold print:** ▨
   - Cut 14 strips 3"w. From these strips, cut 196 **small squares** 3" x 3".
   - Cut 2 **strips** 8"w. From these strips, cut 44 **rectangles** 1¾" x 8".

3. **From green print:** ▨
   - Cut 8 **strips** 3"w.
   - Cut 1 strip 8"w. From this strip, cut 14 **rectangles** 1¾" x 8".
   - Cut 2 strips 4"w. From these strips, cut 18 **border squares** 4" x 4".
   - Cut 2 squares 6¼" x 6¼". Cut squares twice diagonally to make 8 **triangles** (you will need 6 and have 2 left over).
   - Cut 2 **inner border corner squares** 1¾" x 1¾".

4. **From blue print:** ■
   - Cut 8 **strips** 3"w.
   - Cut 1 strip 8"w. From this strip, cut 16 **rectangles** 1¾" x 8".
   - Cut 2 strips 4"w. From these strips, cut 18 **border squares** 4" x 4".
   - Cut 2 squares 6¼" x 6¼". Cut squares twice diagonally to make 8 **triangles** (you will need 6 and have 2 left over).
   - Cut 1 **inner border corner square** 1¾" x 1¾".

5. **From rust print:** ■
   - Cut 8 **strips** 3"w.
   - Cut 1 strip 8"w. From this strip, cut 14 **rectangles** 1¾" x 8".
   - Cut 3 strips 4"w. From these strips, cut 22 **border squares** 4" x 4".
   - Cut 1 square 6¼" x 6¼". Cut square twice diagonally to make 4 **triangles**.
   - Cut 1 **inner border corner square** 1¾" x 1¾".

ASSEMBLING THE QUILT TOP

Follow Piecing and Pressing, page 146, to make quilt top. To simplify assembly, label all units and blocks as they are completed.

1. Place 1 **small square** on each corner of 1 **large square**, matching right sides and raw edges. Stitch diagonally across each small square and trim ¼" from stitching line (**Fig. 1**). Press open to complete **Block A**. Make 49 **Block A's**.

Fig. 1   **Block A** (make 49)

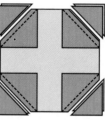

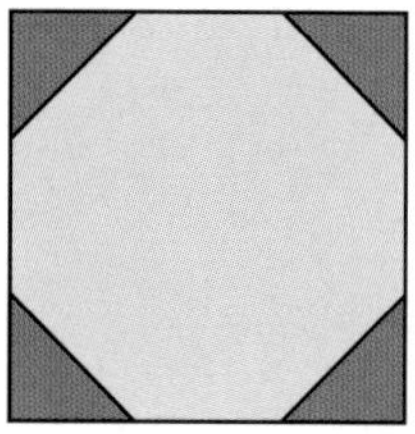

2. Sew 3 **strips** together to make **Strip Set**. Make 2 **Strip Sets**. Cut across **Strip Sets** at 3" intervals to make 20 **Unit 1's**.

Strip Set (make 2)   **Unit 1** (make 20)

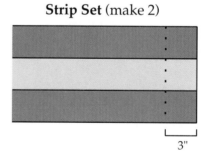

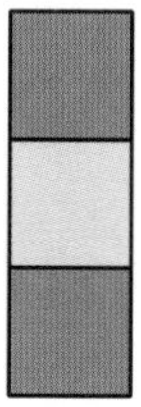

3. Referring to diagrams for color order, make 2 **Strips Sets** as in Step 2 to match each unit. Cut across **Strips Sets** at 3" intervals to make indicated numbers of **Unit 2's - Unit 6's**.

Unit 2	Unit 3	Unit 4	Unit 5	Unit 6
(make 16)	(make 20)	(make 17)	(make 20)	(make 17)

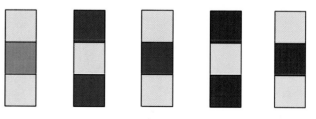

4. Referring to diagrams for color order, make 1 **Strip Set** as in Step 2 to match each unit. Cut across **Strip Sets** at 3" intervals to make indicated numbers of **Unit 7's - Unit 9's.**

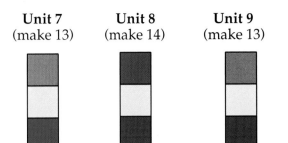

Unit 7 (make 13) Unit 8 (make 14) Unit 9 (make 13)

5. Referring to diagrams for color order, use **Unit 1's - Unit 9's** to make indicated numbers of **Block B's - Block G's.**

Block B (make 10) **Block C** (make 10) **Block D** (make 10)

Block E (make 6) **Block F** (make 7) **Block G** (make 7)

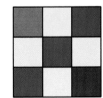

6. Carefully arrange **Blocks** to match **Quilt Top Diagram**, page 44. Sew **Blocks** together into rows, then sew rows together to make center section of quilt top.
7. Referring to diagrams below for color order, sew **rectangles** together to make indicated numbers of **Narrow Borders.**

8. Referring to **Quilt Top Diagram**, sew 1 **Left** and 1 **Right Narrow Border** to center section. Sew 1 **inner border corner square** to each end of 1 **Top** and 1 **Bottom Narrow Border**; sew **Borders** to center section.
9. Referring to diagrams, use **border triangles** and **border squares** to make indicated numbers of **Unit 10's - Unit 12's.**

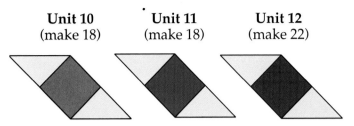

Unit 10 (make 18) Unit 11 (make 18) Unit 12 (make 22)

10. Referring to diagrams, use **triangles** and **border triangles** to make 4 **Unit 13's** and 4 **Unit 14's.**

Unit 13 (make 4) Unit 14 (make 4)

11. Referring to diagrams, use **triangles** and **corner unit triangles** to make 2 **Corner Unit 1's** and 2 **Corner Unit 2's.**

Corner Unit 1 (make 2) Corner Unit 2 (make 2)

12. Referring to **Quilt Top Diagram** for color order, sew 1 **Unit 13**, 6 **Unit 12's**, 5 **Unit 11's**, 5 **Unit 10's**, and 1 **Unit 14** together to make **Side Wide Border**. Make 2 **Side Wide Borders.**
13. Sew 1 **Unit 14**, 5 **Unit 12's**, 4 **Unit 10's**, 4 **Unit 11's**, 1 **Unit 13**, 1 **Corner Unit 1**, and 1 **Corner Unit 2** together to make **Top/Bottom Wide Border**. Make 2 **Top/Bottom Wide Borders.**

Left Narrow Border (make 2)

Right Narrow Border (make 2)

Top Narrow Border (make 2)

Bottom Narrow Border (make 2)

43

14. Sew **Side**, then **Top** and **Bottom Wide Borders** to center section.
15. Sew 1 **rectangle** to each end of each remaining **Narrow Border**.
16. Sew **Left** and **Right Narrow Borders** to center section, aligning seams with those of inner **Narrow Borders** and trimming off remainder of borders at each end after stitching. Repeat to add **Top** and **Bottom Narrow Borders** to complete **Quilt Top**.

COMPLETING THE QUILT

1. Follow **Quilting**, page 151, to mark, layer, and quilt using **Quilting Diagram** as a suggestion. Our quilt is hand quilted.
2. Cut a 34" square of binding fabric. Follow **Binding**, page 155, to bind quilt using 2¹/₂"w bias binding with mitered corners.

Quilting Diagram

Quilt Top Diagram

44

CHANGING SEASONS WALL HANGING

SKILL LEVEL: 1 2 **3** 4 5
BLOCK SIZE: 7¹/₂" x 7¹/₂"
WALL HANGING SIZE: 31" x 31"

YARDAGE REQUIREMENTS
Yardage is based on 45"w fabric.

- ¹/₂ yd of yellow print
- ¹/₂ yd of gold print
- ¹/₄ yd of brown print
- 1 fat quarter (18" x 22" piece) *each* of burgundy print, dark gold print, rust print, dark rust print, 2 green prints, and 2 blue prints
- scrap of small floral print
  1 yd for backing and hanging sleeve
  ³/₈ yd for binding
  34" x 34" batting

You will also need:
  12 red ¹/₄" to ¹/₂" buttons
  paper-backed fusible web
  transparent monofilament thread for appliqué

CUTTING OUT THE PIECES
All measurements include a ¹/₄" seam allowance. Follow **Rotary Cutting**, *page 144, to cut fabric unless otherwise indicated.*

1. **From yellow print:**
    - Cut 4 **large squares** 8" x 8".
    - Cut 1 strip 3"w. From this strip, cut 12 **squares** 3" x 3".
    - Cut 4 **rectangles** 3" x 8".

2. **From gold print:**
    - Cut 2 strips 3"w. From these strips, cut 17 **squares** 3" x 3".
    - Cut 2 strips 4¹/₄"w. From these strips, cut 16 squares 4¹/₄" x 4¹/₄". Cut squares twice diagonally to make 64 **triangles**.
    - Cut 2 squares 3⁷/₈" x 3⁷/₈". Cut squares once diagonally to make 4 **corner unit triangles**.

3. **From brown print:**
    - Cut 2 **top/bottom inner borders** 1¹/₄" x 24¹/₂".
    - Cut 2 **side inner borders** 1¹/₄" x 23".

4. **From rust print, dark rust print, 1 green print, and 1 blue print:**
    - Cut 5 **squares** 3" x 3" from *each* fabric.

5. **From remaining green, blue, rust, gold, and burgundy prints:**
    - Cut a total of 28 **border squares** 2⁵/₈" x 2⁵/₈".
    - Cut a total of 4 squares 4¹/₄" x 4¹/₄". Cut squares twice diagonally to make 16 **border triangles**.

- Referring to photo, use patterns, page 47, and follow **Preparing Fusible Appliqués**, page 149, to cut the following appliqués:
  - 4 **tulips**
  - 4 **tulip leaves**
  - 4 **beets**
  - 4 **beet tops**
  - 4 **oak leaves** (1 in reverse)
  - 4 **trees** (2 in reverse)
  - 12 - 24 **small leaves** for each of 3 trees (1 tree has none)
  - 4 **holly leaves**
  - 3 **holly berries**
  - 2 **acorns**
  - 2 **acorn tops**

6. **From small floral print:**
    - Fuse web to wrong side of fabric. Cut out 12 - 14 **small flowers**, taking advantage of fabric design. Remove paper backing.

ASSEMBLING THE WALL HANGING TOP
Follow **Piecing and Pressing**, *page 146, to make wall hanging top.*

1. Using **large squares** and gold **squares**, follow Step 1 of **Assembling the Quilt Top**, page 42, to make 4 **Block A's**.

2. Sew 3 **squares** together to make **Unit 1**. Make 2 **Unit 1's**. Sew **Unit 1's** and 1 **rectangle** together to make 1 **Block B**.

Unit 1 (make 2)

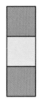

Block B (make 1)

3. Referring to diagrams and using **squares** and **rectangles**, repeat Step 2 to make **Block C - Block F**.

Block C (make 1)

Block D (make 1)

Block E (make 1)

Block F (make 1)

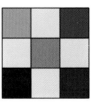

4. Referring to **Wall Hanging Top Diagram**, follow **Invisible Appliqué**, page 150, to stitch appliqués to blocks. Using a coordinating thread, follow **Satin Stitch Appliqué**, page 149, to stitch detail lines on holly leaves and oak leaves.

5. Sew **Blocks** together into rows, then sew rows together to make center section of wall hanging top.

6. Sew **side**, then **top** and **bottom inner borders** to center section.

7. Sew 2 **triangles** and 1 **border square** together to make **Unit 2**. Make 28 **Unit 2's**.

Unit 2 (make 28)

8. Sew 1 **triangle** and 1 **border triangle** together to make **Unit 3**. Make 8 **Unit 3's**.

Unit 3 (make 8)

9. Sew 2 **border triangles** and 1 **corner unit triangle** together to make 1 **Corner Unit**. Make 4 **Corner Units**.

Corner Unit (make 4)

10. Sew together 2 **Unit 3's** and 7 **Unit 2's**, arranged in random color order, to make 1 **Pieced Border**. Make 4 **Pieced Borders**.

Pieced Border (make 4)

11. Sew 1 **Pieced Border** to each side edge of center section. Sew 1 **Corner Unit** to each end of remaining **Pieced Borders**. Sew **Borders** to top and bottom edges of center section to complete **Wall Hanging Top**.

COMPLETING THE WALL HANGING

1. Follow **Quilting**, page 151, to mark, layer, and quilt using **Quilting Diagram** as a suggestion. Our wall hanging is hand quilted.

2. Follow **Making a Hanging Sleeve**, page 157, to attach hanging sleeve to wall hanging.

3. Follow **Binding**, page 155, to bind wall hanging using 2½"w straight-grain binding with mitered corners.

4. Referring to photo, sew buttons to tree in top row of wall hanging.

Quilting Diagram

Wall Hanging Top Diagram

APPLIQUÉD CLOTHING

SUPPLIES

desired garment
scraps of assorted print fabrics for appliqués
paper-backed fusible web
thread to match appliqué fabrics

TRIMMING THE GARMENT

1. Use patterns and follow **Preparing Fusible Appliqués**, page 149, to cut desired appliqués from assorted scrap fabrics.
2. Follow **Satin Stitch Appliqué**, page 149, to stitch each appliqué to garment and to stitch over any detail lines.

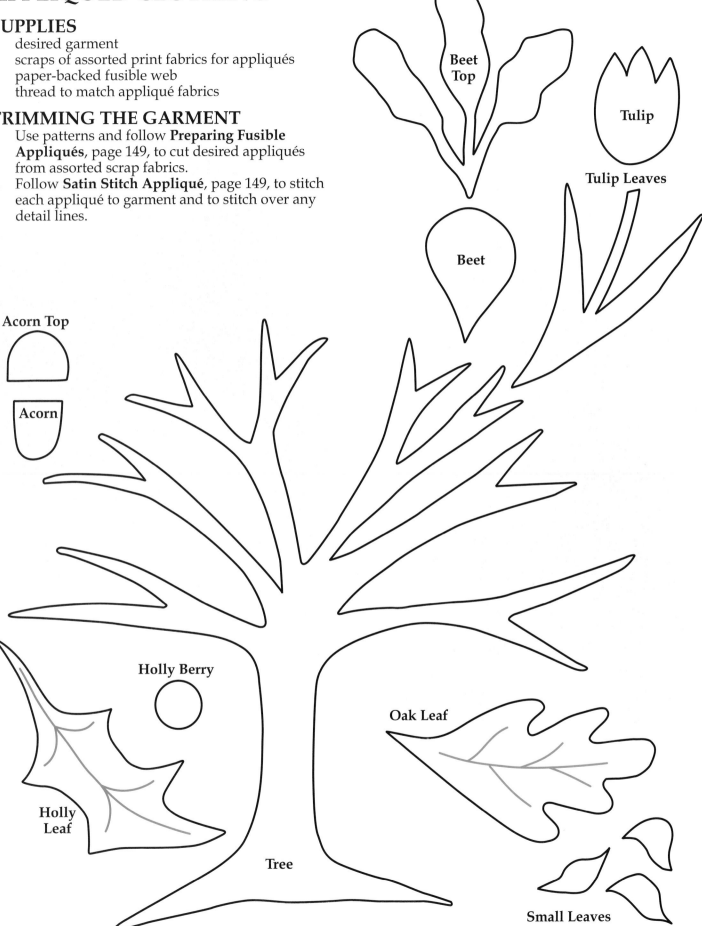

Beet Top

Tulip

Tulip Leaves

Beet

Acorn Top

Acorn

Holly Berry

Oak Leaf

Holly Leaf

Tree

Small Leaves

PLAID GARDEN

The rustic beauty of homespun plaids is a natural complement to the simple blooms on our Plaid Garden quilt. Even though the quilt looks old-fashioned, we used the latest rotary cutting techniques for fast, fun results. Each pieced block is made with rotary-cut strip-set units, and the assortment of Nine-Patch and appliquéd blocks is unified with checked sashing strips and setting squares. For no-fuss appliqués, we fused the motifs in place and used clear nylon thread to machine stitch the edges. Basic machine quilting subtly accents the overall design and provides an extra-easy finish.

PLAID GARDEN QUILT

SKILL LEVEL: 1 2 3 4 5
BLOCK SIZE: 10½" x 10½"
QUILT SIZE: 95" x 108"

YARDAGE REQUIREMENTS
Yardage is based 45"w fabric.

- ■ 4 yds of medium plaid for sashing strips
- ◩ 1⅜ yds *each* of 3 light plaids for background blocks
- ■ ⅞ yd of green plaid for leaf and stem appliqués
- ■ ⅝ yd of dark plaid for sashing squares
- ▢ ½ yd *each* of 3 light plaids for nine-patch blocks
- ◪ ¼ yd *each* of 9 dark plaids for nine-patch blocks
- ▨ ⅛ yd of gold print for flower center appliqués
- ◩ scraps of assorted plaids for flower appliqués
  8⅝ yds for backing
  1 yd for binding
  120" x 120" batting

You will also need:
 paper-backed fusible web
 transparent monofilament thread for appliqué

CUTTING OUT THE PIECES
All measurements include a ¼" seam allowance. Follow Rotary Cutting, page 144, to cut fabric.

1. **From medium plaid for sashing strips:** ■
    - Cut 43 strips 3"w. From these strips, cut 127 **sashing strips** 3" x 11".

2. **From *each* of 3 light plaids for background blocks:** ◩
    - Cut 10 **background strips** 4"w.

3. **From dark plaid for sashing squares:** ■
    - Cut 6 strips 3"w. From these strips, cut 72 **sashing squares** 3" x 3".

4. **From light plaids for nine-patch blocks:** ▢
    - Cut 112 **squares** 4" x 4". You will need 28 sets of 4 matching light plaid squares.

5. **From dark plaids for nine-patch blocks:** ◪
    - Cut 140 **squares** 4" x 4". You will need 28 sets of 1 different and 4 matching dark plaid squares.

PREPARING THE APPLIQUÉS
Use patterns, page 53, and follow Preparing Fusible Appliqués, page 149, to cut appliqués.

1. **From green plaid for leaf and stem appliqués:** ■
    - Cut 28 **stems** (12 in reverse).
    - Cut 56 **leaves** (28 in reverse).

2. **From assorted plaids for flower appliqués:** ◩
    - Cut 28 **flowers**.

3. **From gold print for flower center appliqués:** ▨
    - Cut 28 **flower centers**.

ASSEMBLING THE QUILT TOP
Follow Piecing and Pressing, page 146, to make quilt top.

1. Sew 1 set of light plaid **squares** and 1 set of dark plaid **squares** together to make **Nine-Patch Block**. Make 28 **Nine-Patch Blocks**.

Nine-Patch Block (make 28)

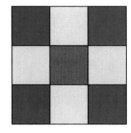

2. Sew 3 different **background strips** together to make **Strip Set**. Make 10 **Strip Sets**. Cut across **Strip Sets** at 11" intervals to make 28 **Background Blocks**.

Strip Set
(make 10)

Background Block
(make 28)

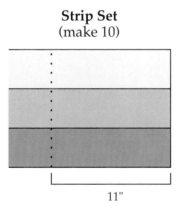

11"

3. Follow **Invisible Appliqué**, page 150, to stitch appliqués to **Background Blocks** to make 12 **Flower Block A's** and 16 **Flower Block B's**.

Flower Block A
(make 12)

Flower Block B
(make 16)

4. Sew 8 **sashing squares** and 7 **sashing strips** together to make **Sashing Row**. Make 9 **Sashing Rows**.
5. Sew 8 **sashing strips**, 4 **Nine-Patch Blocks**, and 3 **Flower Block A's** together to make **Row A**. Make 4 **Row A's**.
6. Sew 8 **sashing strips**, 4 **Flower Block B's**, and 3 **Nine-Patch Blocks** together to make **Row B**. Make 4 **Row B's**.
7. Refer to **Quilt Top Diagram**, page 52, to sew **Sashing Rows**, **Row A's**, and **Row B's** together to complete **Quilt Top**.

COMPLETING THE QUILT

1. Follow **Quilting**, page 151, to mark, layer, and quilt using **Quilting Diagram** as a suggestion. Our quilt is machine quilted.
2. Cut a 34" square of binding fabric. Follow **Binding**, page 155, to bind quilt using 2¹/₂"w straight-grain binding with mitered corners.

Quilting Diagram

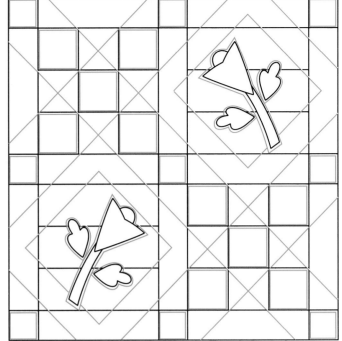

Sashing Row (make 9)

Row A (make 4)

Row B (make 4)

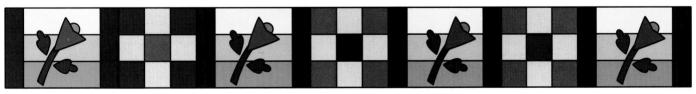

51

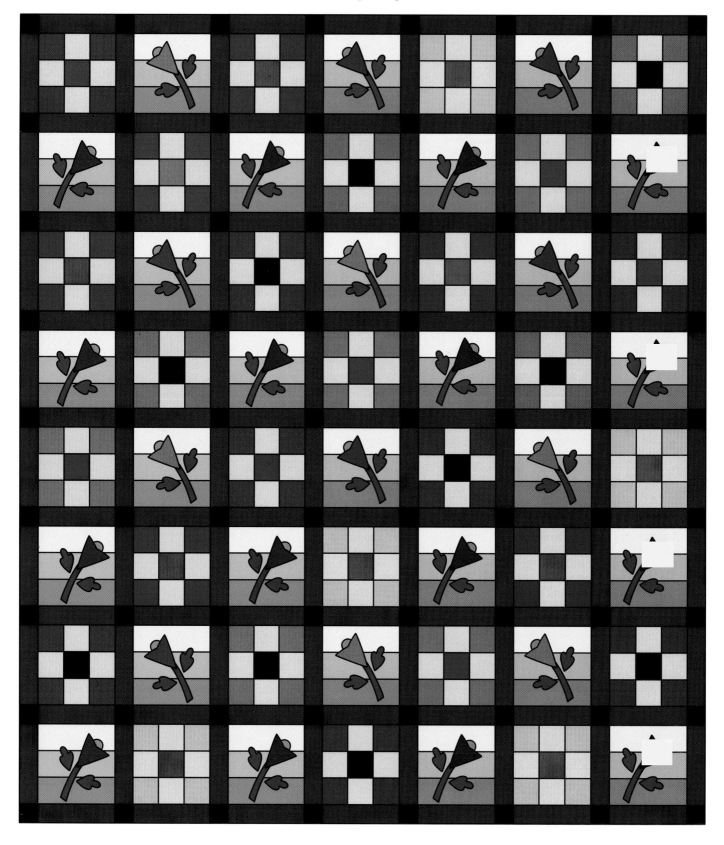

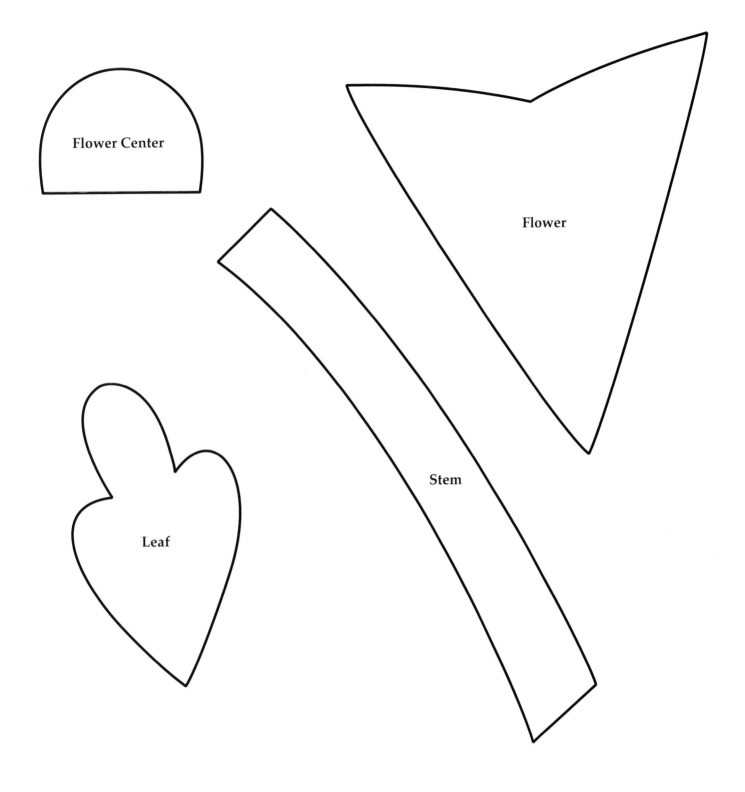

Flower Center

Flower

Stem

Leaf

NINE-PATCH MANTEL SCARF

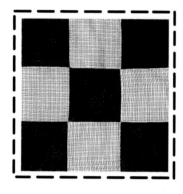

Draped with our simple Nine-Patch mantel scarf, your fireplace will glow with rustic charm. You'll find it easy to customize the length of the scarf to fit any size mantel. And this project is especially carefree to assemble because there's no binding — just sew the front and back pieces together with a layer of batting and then turn the scarf right side out. Machine quilted for a fast finish, this quaint accent is so quick to create, it's the perfect project for a hectic schedule!

NINE-PATCH MANTEL SCARF

BLOCK SIZE: 6" x 6"

SUPPLIES

 light tan print fabric for scarf panel and setting pieces

scraps of light and dark print fabrics for nine-patch blocks

fabric for backing

batting

MAKING THE MANTEL SCARF

*Follow **Rotary Cutting**, page 144, and **Piecing and Pressing**, page 146, to make mantel scarf.*

1. Measure length and width of mantel as shown in **Fig. 1**. Round length measurement down to a number divisible by $8\frac{1}{2}$ to determine finished scarf length measurement.

Fig. 1

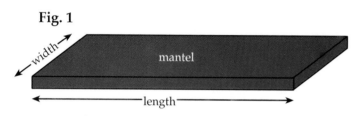

2. To cut out scarf panel, add $\frac{1}{2}$" to finished length measurement; add $\frac{1}{2}$" to width measurement. From light tan print fabric, cut **scarf panel** the determined measurements.

3. Divide finished scarf length measurement (determined in Step 1) by $8\frac{1}{2}$ to determine the number of nine-patch blocks to make.

4. For each nine-patch block, cut 5 squares $2\frac{1}{2}$" x $2\frac{1}{2}$" from 1 dark print fabric and 4 squares $2\frac{1}{2}$" x $2\frac{1}{2}$" from 1 light print fabric. Sew squares together to make **Nine-Patch Block**.

Nine-Patch Block

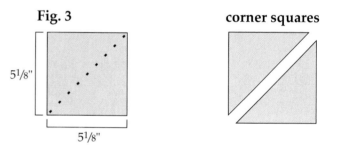

5. Subtract 1 from the number of Nine-Patch Blocks (determined in Step 3) to determine the number of setting triangles needed.

6. From light tan print fabric, cut 1 square $9\frac{3}{4}$" x $9\frac{3}{4}$". Cut square twice diagonally to make 4 **setting triangles (Fig. 2)**. Repeat to cut additional **setting triangles** if needed.

Fig. 2   **setting triangles**

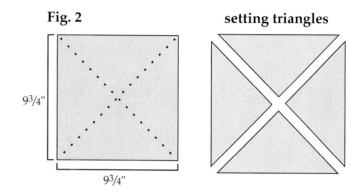

7. From light tan print fabric, cut 1 square $5\frac{1}{8}$" x $5\frac{1}{8}$". Cut square once diagonally to make 2 **corner squares (Fig. 3)**.

Fig. 3   **corner squares**

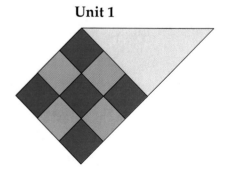

8. Sew 1 **Nine-Patch Block** and 1 **setting triangle** together to make **Unit 1**.

Unit 1

9. Sew remaining **Nine-Patch Blocks** and **setting triangles** to **Unit 1** to make **Unit 2**.

Unit 2

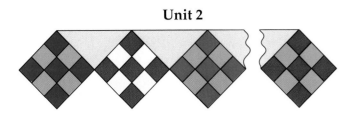

10. Sew **corner squares** to each end of **Unit 2** to make **Scarf Drop**.

Scarf Drop

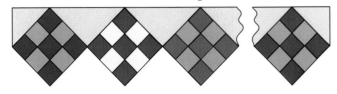

11. Referring to **Mantel Scarf Top Diagram**, sew **scarf panel** to **Scarf Drop** to make **Mantel Scarf Top**.
12. Cut 1 rectangle each from backing fabric and batting 2" larger than mantel scarf top.

13. Place backing right side up on top of batting. Center mantel scarf top wrong side up on backing. Using a $1/4$" seam allowance, sew top, backing, and batting together, leaving a 6" opening for turning. Trim backing and batting close to seamline. Cut corners diagonally and clip inside angles. Turn right side out; press. Blindstitch opening closed.
14. Follow **Machine Quilting**, page 154, to quilt mantel scarf using **Quilting Diagram** as a suggestion.

Quilting Diagram

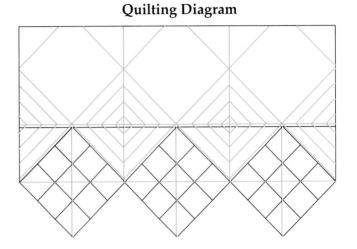

Mantel Scarf Top Diagram

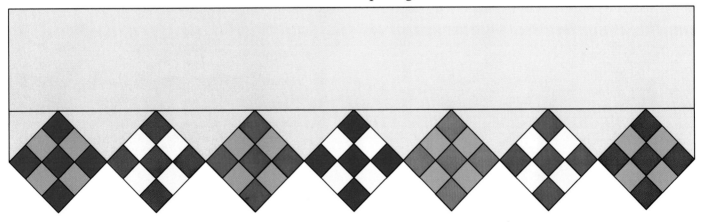

BASKET COLLECTION

Basket motifs and a classic color scheme give this collection the old-fashioned mood of quilts from the 1800's. Treasured for their simple beauty, as well as for their practical importance in the home, the carry-alls were often depicted on quilts. For our homey spread and coordinating accessories, we chose a sewing basket theme to reflect the integral part that needlework played in the lives of women in those days. The triangle-squares creating the pieced blocks are easy to make using a grid method. Dark blue pindot and star prints re-create the look of the indigo-dyed cloth favored long ago.

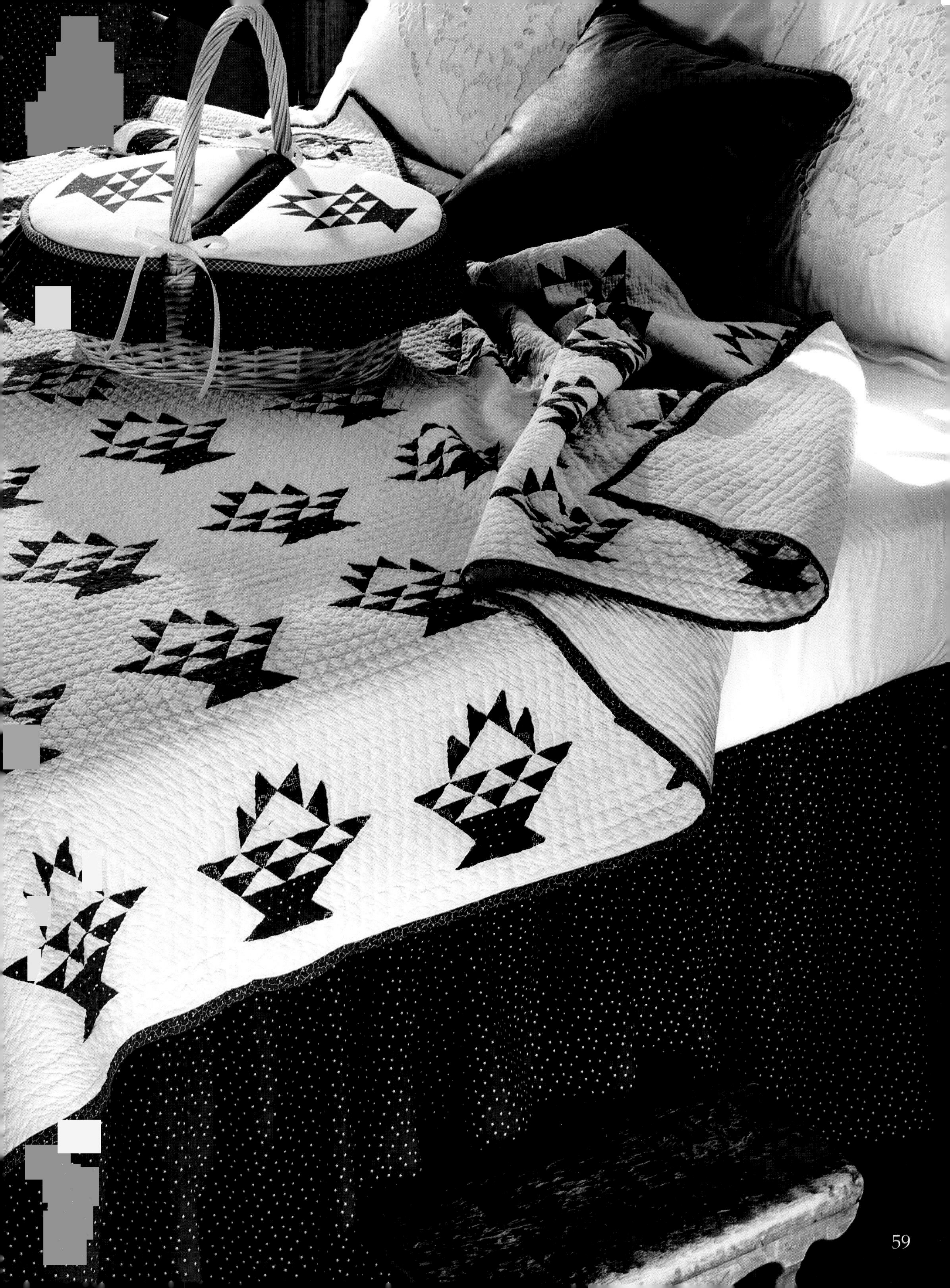

Embellished with basket motifs, our charming hope chest will add a coordinating touch to the bedroom when paired with the cozy coverlet. The padded panel is easy to make using fused-on appliqués. Dark blue welting and ribbon trim provide the finishing touches. Reminiscent of the trunks once used by adolescent girls to protect their dowry of quilt tops, the chest is ideal for storing cherished keepsakes.

In olden days, a young lady's sewing basket and accessories were never far away. Our charming set (left) includes a plump pincushion and a handy chatelaine to keep needles and scissors at your fingertips. Dressed up with a padded cardboard lid decorated with no-sew basket motifs, the roomy basket (below) will be a fitting place for all your needlework supplies!

BASKET QUILT

SKILL LEVEL: 1 2 *3* 4 5
BLOCK SIZE: 5⅝" x 5⅝"
QUILT SIZE: 65" x 89"

To make the fastest possible basket block, we used a single navy print and changed the construction of the basket base slightly.

YARDAGE REQUIREMENTS
Yardage is based on 45"w fabric.

☐ 6⅞ yds of white solid

■ 2¾ yds of navy print
5½ yds for backing
1 yd for binding
81" x 96" batting

CUTTING OUT THE PIECES
All measurements include a ¼" seam allowance. Follow Rotary Cutting, page 144, to cut fabric.

1. **From white solid:** ☐
    *   Cut 12 strips 6⅛"w. From these strips, cut 70 **setting squares** 6⅛" x 6⅛".
    *   Cut 3 strips 9¼"w. From these strips, cut 9 squares 9¼" x 9¼". Cut squares twice diagonally to make 36 **setting triangles** (you will need 34 and have 2 left over).
    *   Cut 4 strips 3⅛"w. From these strips, cut 44 squares 3⅛" x 3⅛". Cut squares once diagonally to make 88 **medium triangles**.
    *   Cut 4 strips 1⅝"w. From these strips, cut 88 **small squares** 1⅝" x 1⅝".
    *   Cut 18 strips 1⅝"w. From these strips, cut 176 **small rectangles** 1⅝" x 3⅞".
    *   Cut 6 **large squares** 20" x 20" for small triangle-squares.
    *   Cut 2 **large rectangles** 14" x 20" for large triangle-squares.
    *   Cut 2 squares 4⅞" x 4⅞". Cut squares once diagonally to make 4 **corner setting triangles**.

2. **From navy print:** ■
    *   Cut 5 strips 2"w. From these strips, cut 88 squares 2" x 2". Cut squares once diagonally to make 176 **small triangles**.
    *   Cut 6 **large squares** 20" x 20" for small triangle-squares.
    *   Cut 2 **large rectangles** 14" x 20" for large triangle-squares.

ASSEMBLING THE QUILT TOP
Follow Piecing and Pressing, page 146, to make quilt top.

1. To make small triangle-squares, place 1 navy and 1 white **large square** right sides together. Referring to **Fig. 1** and starting and stopping stitching as necessary, follow **Making Triangle-Squares**, page 147, to complete 162 **small triangle-squares**.

Repeat with remaining **large squares** to make a total of 972 **small triangle-squares** (you will need 968 and have 4 left over).

Fig. 1

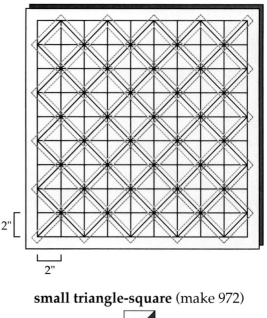

small triangle-square (make 972)

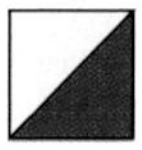

2. To make large triangle-squares, place 1 navy and 1 white **large rectangle** right sides together. Referring to **Fig. 2** and starting and stopping stitching as necessary, follow **Making Triangle-Squares**, page 147, to complete 48 **large triangle-squares**. Repeat with remaining **large rectangles** to make 96 **large triangle-squares** (you will need 88 and have 8 left over).

Fig. 2

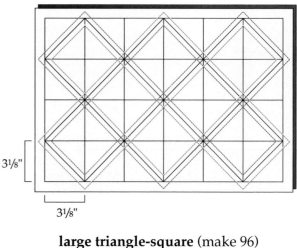

large triangle-square (make 96)

3. Sew 2 **small triangle-squares** together to make **Unit 1**. Make 88 **Unit 1's**.

Unit 1 (make 88)

4. Sew 2 **small triangles**, 1 **small triangle-square**, and 1 **medium triangle** together to make **Unit 2**. Make 88 **Unit 2's**.

Unit 2 (make 88)

5. Sew 1 **small square** and 2 **small triangle-squares** together to make **Unit 3**. Make 88 **Unit 3's**.

Unit 3 (make 88)

6. Sew 1 **Unit 1**, 1 **Unit 2**, and 1 **Unit 3** together to make **Unit 4**. Make 88 **Unit 4's**.

Unit 4 (make 88)

7. Sew 1 **small rectangle** and 3 **small triangle-squares** together to make **Unit 5**. Make 88 **Unit 5's**. Sew 3 **small triangle-squares** and 1 **small rectangle** together to make **Unit 6**. Make 88 **Unit 6's**.

Unit 5 (make 88)   Unit 6 (make 88)

8. Sew 1 **Unit 5**, 1 **Unit 4**, 1 **large triangle-square**, and 1 **Unit 6** together to make **Block**. Make 88 **Blocks**.

Block (make 88)

9. Referring to **Assembly Diagram**, sew **corner setting triangles**, **setting triangles**, **Blocks**, and **setting squares** together into rows. Sew rows together to complete **Quilt Top**.

COMPLETING THE QUILT

1. Follow **Quilting**, page 151, to mark, layer, and quilt. Our quilt is hand quilted in a small grid pattern.
2. Cut a 30" square of binding fabric. Follow **Binding**, page 155, to bind quilt using 2$\frac{1}{2}$"w bias binding with mitered corners.

Assembly Diagram

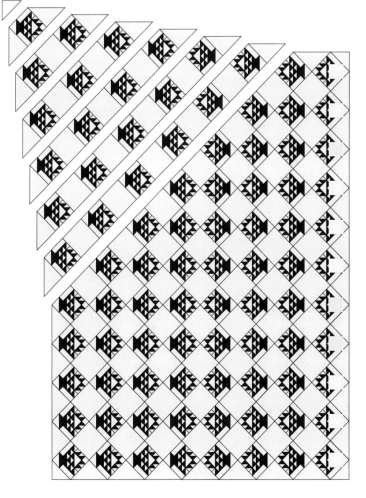

HOPE CHEST WITH PADDED PANEL

PANEL SIZE: 9" x 26"

We purchased our chest at an unfinished furniture store, applied a pickling stain and varnish, and then added a padded panel for the finishing touch.

SUPPLIES

1 yd of 45"w navy plaid fabric
scraps of white solid, navy solid, and navy print fabrics
2 yds of 2"w bias fabric strip for welting
8" x 24³/₄" batting
4 yds of ¹/₄"w navy grosgrain ribbon
2 yds of ¹/₄" cord for welting
heavy-duty paper-backed fusible web
medium weight fusible interfacing
8¹/₄" x 25" piece of corrugated cardboard
hot glue gun and glue sticks

CUTTING OUT THE PIECES

1. Follow manufacturer's instructions to apply interfacing to wrong side of white solid fabric.
2. Follow manufacturer's instructions to fuse web to wrong sides of white solid, navy solid, and navy print.
3. Follow **Rotary Cutting**, page 144, to cut pieces indicated below.
   From navy plaid:
   • Cut 1 **background** 12" x 29" on the bias.
   From white solid:
   • Cut 3 **squares** 5⁷/₈" x 5⁷/₈".
   From navy solid:
   • Cut 20 squares 1¹/₈" x 1¹/₈". Cut squares once diagonally to make 40 **small triangles** (you will need 39 and have 1 left over).
   From navy print:
   • Cut 2 squares 2¹/₄" x 2¹/₄". Cut squares once diagonally to make 4 **medium triangles** (you will need 3 and have 1 left over).

MAKING THE PADDED PANEL

1. Center batting, then cardboard on wrong side of **background**.
2. Alternating sides and pulling fabric taut, glue edges of fabric to back of cardboard to complete **panel**, folding fabric as necessary at corners.
3. Remove paper backing from **small** and **medium triangles** only. Referring to **Block** diagram, page 63, and photo, arrange **triangles** on **squares**, leaving ¹/₈" around edges of squares to be covered by ribbon; fuse in place.
4. Remove paper backing from **squares**. Center and fuse **squares** to **panel** with inner corners touching.

5. Cut ribbon into 18" lengths. Referring to photo, center and glue ribbon over edges of squares. Fold ribbon ends to back of cardboard and glue in place.
6. Lay cord along center of bias strip on wrong side of fabric; fold strip over cord. Using a zipper foot, machine baste along length of strip close to cord to make welting.
7. Beginning and ending 3" from end of welting, glue flange of welting to wrong side of **panel** along edge.
8. Refer to Step 4 of **Adding Welting to Pillow Top**, page 158, to finish welting ends; glue to panel.
9. Glue **panel** to front of chest.

PRETTY PINCUSHION

SUPPLIES

11¹/₂" x 11¹/₂" square *each* of navy print and white solid fabrics
9" x 9" square of lining fabric
11" x 11" square of white flannel
30" of ¹/₂"w navy grosgrain ribbon
4" plastic foam ball
paring knife
craft glue
compass
tracing paper

MAKING THE PINCUSHION

*Follow **Piecing and Pressing**, page 146, to make pincushion.*

1. To make triangle-squares, place navy and white squares right sides together. Referring to **Fig. 1**, follow **Making Triangle-Squares**, page 147, to make 50 **triangle-squares** (you will need 49 and have 1 left over).

Fig. 1

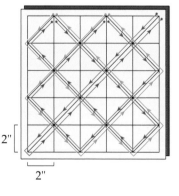

triangle-square (make 50)

2. Sew 49 **triangle-squares** together to make **Unit 1**.

Unit 1 (make 1)

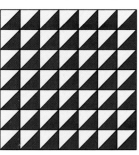

3. For patterns, use compass to draw an 8" circle and a 10¹/₂" circle on tracing paper; cut out.
4. Use patterns to cut 1 small circle each from **Unit 1** and lining fabric and to cut 1 large circle from flannel.
5. Use knife to cut 1" from foam ball, forming a flat surface (bottom). Center and glue flannel circle over rounded part (top) of ball, smoothing wrinkles as necessary. Secure with pins until glue is dry.
6. Matching right sides and raw edges, sew small fabric circles together. Clip seam allowance and cut a slit in center of lining only; turn right side out and press.
7. Using heavy thread, hand baste ⁵/₈" from edge of circle. Center ball on lining. Pull basting thread, gathering fabric around ball; knot thread and trim ends. Glue lining to ball along basting line.
8. Tie a knot at center of ribbon. Tie a knot 3" from each side of center knot. Tie ribbon into a bow around pincushion, covering basting thread. Use dots of glue behind knots and bow to secure.

CHATELAINE

SUPPLIES
¹/₂ yd of 45"w white solid fabric
¹/₄ yd of 45"w navy print fabric
2" x 2¹/₂" piece of white felt
30" of ³/₈"w navy grosgrain ribbon
1 yd of 1³/₄"w bias strip for binding
scraps of low-loft batting
tracing paper
fabric glue

MAKING THE CHATELAINE
Follow **Piecing and Pressing**, *page 146, to make chatelaine.*

SCISSORS CARRIER
1. For back pattern, trace blue outline of pattern onto tracing paper. For pocket pattern, trace grey area of pattern onto tracing paper. Cut out patterns.
2. Use patterns to cut 2 backs and 2 pockets from white solid and 1 back and 1 pocket from batting.
3. With right sides facing out, place 1 back on each side of back batting; baste around edges. Repeat with pocket pieces.

4. Cut one 3¹/₈" length of bias strip; press in half lengthwise, wrong sides together. Follow Steps 1 and 3 of **Attaching Binding with Overlapped Corners**, page 157, to bind top edge of pocket.
5. Matching bottom and side edges, baste back and pocket pieces together.
6. To bind edges of carrier, cut one 17" length of bias strip. Press 1 end of strip ¹/₂" to wrong side. Press strip in half lengthwise with wrong sides together. Follow Step 1 of **Attaching Binding with Overlapped Corners**, page 157, covering raw end of binding with pressed end.
7. For ties, cut two 6" lengths of ribbon. Press 1 end of each length ¹/₄" to 1 side. With scissors carrier open, whipstitch pressed end of 1 tie to center top edge of flap on outside of carrier. Fold flap closed where indicated on pattern by blue dotted line; whipstitch pressed end of remaining tie to pocket opposite tie on flap.

NEEDLE CASE
1. Cut two 3" x 6" pieces from white solid and one 3" x 6" piece from batting. With right sides facing out, place 1 fabric piece on each side of batting; baste around edges.
2. For center fold line, match short edges and press needle case in half; unfold. Stitch along pressed line.
3. For needle holder, center felt on right half of lining; glue top ¹/₂" of felt in place.
4. Cut one 25" length of bias strip. Press in half lengthwise, wrong sides together. Follow **Attaching Binding with Mitered Corners**, page 156, to bind edges of needle case.
5. For ties, cut one 18" length of ribbon. Center ribbon lengthwise on outside of opened needle case; glue in place.

PIECED RIBBON
1. To make triangle-squares, cut one 7¹/₂" x 11¹/₂" rectangle each from navy print and white solid fabrics. Place rectangles right sides together. Referring to **Fig. 1**, follow **Making Triangle-Squares**, page 147, to make 30 **triangle-squares**.

Fig. 1

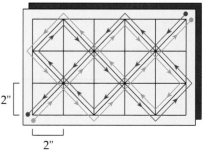

triangle-square (make 30)

2. Referring to photo, sew triangle-squares together end to end to make pieced ribbon front.

3. From white solid, cut 1 back 1⅝" x 34¼". Sew front and back together along long edges. Turn right side out and press to make pieced ribbon.

4. Press ends of pieced ribbon ¼" to right side. With right side of pieced ribbon facing back of scissors carrier, securely sew pieced ribbon to carrier. Repeat to attach remaining end of pieced ribbon to back of needle case.

BASKET WITH PADDED LID

SUPPLIES
basket with handle
white solid fabric for lid
scraps of 2 navy print fabrics for lid appliqués
navy print fabric for lid lining, fabric hinge,
    pleated ruffle, basket lining, and padded bottom
navy plaid fabric for welting
batting
paper-backed fusible web
½" cord for welting
1½ yds of ⅜"w white grosgrain ribbon
corrugated cardboard
poster board
hot glue gun and glue sticks
Hot Tape™ heat-resistant tape

MAKING THE PADDED LID
1. For basket lid, place edge of cardboard even with table edge. Refer to **Fig. 1** to draw around each end of basket on cardboard. Cut pieces from cardboard.

Fig. 1

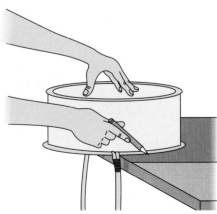

2. For lid lining, cut 2 pieces from poster board same size as cardboard pieces. From navy print, cut 2 pieces 1" larger on all sides than poster board pieces. Set lid lining pieces aside.

3. Cut 2 pieces from white solid 1½" larger on all sides than cardboard pieces. Cut 2 pieces of batting slightly smaller than cardboard pieces.

4. Center 1 batting piece, then 1 cardboard piece on wrong side of 1 white solid piece. Alternating sides and pulling fabric taut, glue edges of fabric to back of cardboard. Repeat for remaining lid piece.

5. For lid appliqués, cut one 7" square from 1 navy print scrap and one 4" square from remaining navy print scrap. Follow manufacturer's instructions to fuse web to wrong sides of squares.

6. From 7" square, cut 13 squares 1⅛" x 1⅛". Cut squares once diagonally to make 26 small triangles. Remove paper backing.

7. From 4" square, cut 1 square 2¼" x 2¼". Cut square once diagonally to make 2 large triangles. Remove paper backing.

8. Referring to **Block** diagram, page 63, and photo, arrange triangles on center of each padded lid piece; fuse in place.

9. For welting, measure curved edge of 1 padded lid piece. Cut a length of cord the determined measurement. Add 2" to cord measurement and cut a 2¾"w bias strip from navy plaid the determined measurement. Follow Step 2 of **Adding Welting to Pillow Top**, page 158, to make welting, leaving 1" of bias strip empty at each end.

10. Beginning 1" from end of welting, glue flange of welting along curved edge on wrong side of padded lid piece. Fold ends of welting to wrong side of lid piece and glue in place (**Fig. 2**).

Fig. 2

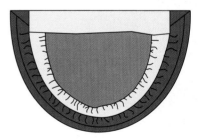

11. Repeat Steps 9 and 10 for remaining padded lid piece.

12. To make hinge, measure width of basket between ends of handle; add 1". Measure width of handle; add 2½". Cut 2 strips of navy print fabric the determined measurement. Press short edges of each hinge fabric piece ½" to wrong side.

13. Cut ribbon in half. Refer to **Fig. 3** to fold each ribbon length in half. On wrong side of 1 hinge fabric piece, glue folded edge of 1 ribbon to each pressed edge.

Fig. 3

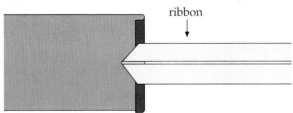

14. Matching wrong sides, glue hinge fabric pieces together.
15. Measure width of handle; add 1". Place padded lid pieces wrong side up with straight edges the determined distance apart. Center fabric hinge over space between lid pieces and glue long edges of hinge to lid pieces (**Fig. 4**).

Fig. 4

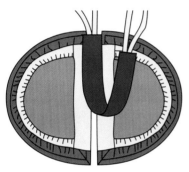

16. For each lid lining piece, center 1 poster board piece on wrong side of 1 fabric piece (cut in Step 2). Alternating sides and pulling fabric taut, glue fabric to back of poster board. Glue 1 lid lining piece to back of each side of lid, keeping ribbons free.
17. For rim measurement, measure around inner edge of basket rim between ends of handle on 1 end of basket. Multiply rim measurement by 2¹/₂ to determine length of pleated ruffle. For width of pleated ruffle, measure from top edge of basket to desired ruffle length; multiply by 2 and add 1¹/₂". Cut 2 strips from navy print fabric the determined measurements.

18. To make pleated ruffle, press 1 short end of 1 strip ¹/₂" to wrong side. Press strip in half lengthwise with wrong sides together. Refer to **Fig. 5** to press 1" pleats with a ¹/₄" overlap, using Hot Tape to hold pleats in place. Add ¹/₂" to rim measurement determined in Step 17; cut pleated strip. Press short raw edge ¹/₂" to wrong side. Repeat with remaining fabric strip.

Fig. 5

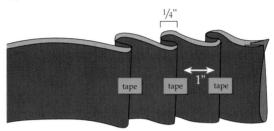

19. Beginning on 1 side of handle, glue long raw edge of 1 pleated strip to inner edge of basket rim ³/₄" below upper edge. Fold pleated strip over top edge of basket; glue in place if necessary. Remove Hot Tape. Repeat for remaining side of basket.
20. To determine width of lining fabric, measure height of basket at highest part; add 2¹/₂". To determine length, measure circumference of basket at widest part; add 2". Cut a piece from navy print fabric the determined measurements. Press 1 long edge and 1 short edge ¹/₂" to wrong side.
21. Beginning with short raw edge, glue long pressed edge along inner edge of basket rim over edge of pleated strip. Overlap short edges and glue in place.
22. For padded bottom, place basket on cardboard and draw around bottom of basket. Cut out cardboard approximately ¹/₂" inside drawn line. Trim to fit in bottom of basket if necessary.
23. Cut a piece of batting the same size as cardboard piece. Cut a piece from navy print fabric 1¹/₂" larger on all sides than cardboard piece.
24. Center batting, then cardboard on wrong side of basket lining fabric. Alternating sides and pulling fabric taut, glue edges of fabric to back of cardboard.
25. Glue padded bottom to inside of basket.
26. To complete basket, place lid on basket and tie ribbons into bows around handles.

TRUE HEART WALL HANGING

Before the mid-1800's, heart patterns were strictly reserved for the bride-to-be and her wedding quilt. Legend held that a girl who used the motif for any other design would never marry at all — an upsetting possibility for women of that era. Our darling wall hanging, featuring a quartet of patchwork hearts, will be a dear keepsake for a bride (or for anyone who enjoys a touch of romance). Accented with simple strip-pieced sashing, the blocks are created with a speedy mock hand appliqué technique. Organdy and machine blindstitch are used to finish the raw edges of the hearts with the look of hand appliqué. Traditional quilting and basic binding make this piece a truly heartwarming project.

TRUE HEART WALL HANGING

SKILL LEVEL: 1 2 3 4 5
BLOCK SIZE: 9" x 9"
WALL HANGING SIZE: 40" x 40"

*To use our speedy mock hand appliqué technique, your sewing machine should have blindstitch capability with a **variable** stitch width. If your blindstitch width cannot be adjusted, you may still wish to try this technique to see if you are satisfied with the results. Some sewing machines have a narrower blindstitch width than others.*

YARDAGE REQUIREMENTS
Yardage is based on 45"w fabric.

■ 1 yd of blue print
■ 1/2 yd of pink solid
■ 1/8 yd of blue solid
◩ scraps of assorted pastel prints
　1/4 yd of organdy or other very lightweight cotton fabric
　11/2 yds for backing and hanging sleeve
　3/8 yd for binding
　44" x 44" batting

You will also need:
　transparent monofilament thread for appliqué
　pinking shears (optional)

CUTTING OUT THE PIECES
*All measurements include a 1/4" seam allowance. Follow **Rotary Cutting**, page 144, to cut fabric.*

1. **From blue print:** ■
   - Cut 4 strips 5"w for **borders**.
   - Cut 4 **wide strips** 21/2"w.

2. **From pink solid:** ■
   - Cut 8 **narrow strips** 11/2"w.
   - Cut 1 **wide strip** 21/2"w.

3. **From blue solid:** ■
   - Cut 2 **narrow strips** 11/2"w.

4. **From assorted print scraps for blocks:** ◩
   - Cut a total of 32 **squares** 5" x 5".

ASSEMBLING THE WALL HANGING TOP
*Follow **Piecing and Pressing**, page 146, to make wall hanging top.*

PREPARING THE APPLIQUÉS
1. Sew 4 **squares** together to make **Unit 1**. Make 8 **Unit 1's**. (You will need 4 Unit 1's to make heart appliqués and 4 Unit 1's for block backgrounds.)

Unit 1 (make 8)

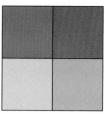

2. Use heart pattern, page 73, to trace 4 **hearts** onto wrong side of organdy, leaving at least 1" between drawn hearts. Cut out organdy hearts at least 1/2" outside outer marked lines.

3. Referring to **Fig. 1**, place 1 organdy heart and 1 **Unit 1** right sides together, lining up straight lines on heart with Unit 1 seamlines. Sew pieces together along outer marked line. Trim point and clip inside curves; use pinking shears to trim heart seam allowances to 1/8" (trim to 1/4" and clip curves if not using pinking shears).

Fig. 1

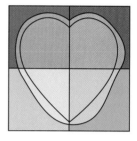

4. To make an opening for turning, cut a slit in organdy only (**Fig. 2**). Turn right side out and press to make **Heart Appliqué**. Make 4 **Heart Appliqués**.

Fig. 2

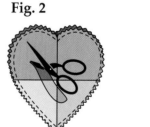

Heart Appliqué (make 4)

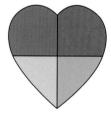

MAKING THE BLOCKS
1. Thread needle of sewing machine with transparent monofilament thread; use general-purpose thread in bobbin in a neutral color to blend with background fabrics.

2. Set sewing machine for narrow blindstitch (just wide enough to catch 2 or 3 threads of the appliqué) and a very short stitch length (20 - 30 stitches per inch).

3. Referring to **Block** diagram, place 1 **Heart Appliqué** right side up on 1 **Unit 1**, lining up seamlines. Use pins or hand baste to secure.

4. (*Note:* Follow Steps 5 - 8 of **Satin Stitch Appliqué**, page 149, for needle position when pivoting.) Starting on 1 side edge, sew around edges of each **Heart Appliqué** so that the straight stitches fall on the background fabric very near the appliqué and the "hem" stitches barely catch the folded edge of the appliqué (**Fig. 3**). At bottom of heart, switch machine setting to zigzag stitch to secure point, then return setting to blindstitch for remainder of stitching.

Fig. 3

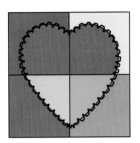

5. It is not necessary to backstitch at the beginning or end of stitching. End stitching by sewing ¹/₄" over the first stitches. Trim thread ends close to fabric to complete **Block**.

Block (make 4)

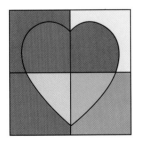

6. To reduce bulk, turn **Block** over and use scissors to cut away background fabric and organdy approximately ¹/₄" inside stitching line of appliqué as shown in **Fig. 4**.

Fig. 4

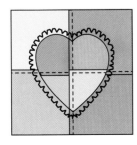

7. Repeat Steps 3 - 6 to make 4 **Blocks**.

MAKING THE SASHING

1. Sew 2 **narrow strips** and 1 **wide strip** together to make **Strip Set A**. Make 4 **Strip Set A's**.

Strip Set A (make 4)

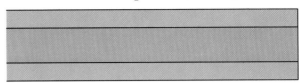

2. Cut across **Strip Set A's** at 9¹/₂" intervals to make 12 **Sashing Unit 1's**. Cut across remainder of **Strip Set A's** at 2¹/₂" intervals to make 9 **Sashing Unit 2's**.

Sashing Unit 1 (make 12)   **Sashing Unit 2** (make 9)

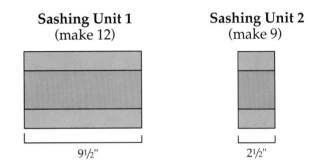

9¹/₂"   2¹/₂"

3. Sew 2 **narrow strips** and 1 **wide strip** together to make 1 **Strip Set B**. Cut across **Strip Set B** at 1¹/₂" intervals to make 18 **Sashing Unit 3's**.

Strip Set B (make 1)   **Sashing Unit 3** (make 18)

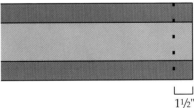

1¹/₂"

ASSEMBLING THE WALL HANGING TOP

1. Sew 2 **Sashing Unit 1's**, 3 **Sashing Unit 2's**, and 6 **Sashing Unit 3's** together to make **Sashing Row**. Make 3 **Sashing Rows**.

Sashing Row (make 3)

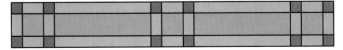

2. Sew 3 **Sashing Unit 1's** and 2 **Blocks** together to make **Block Row**. Make 2 **Block Rows**.

Block Row (make 2)

3. Referring to **Wall Hanging Top Diagram**, sew **Rows** together to make center section of wall hanging top.
4. Follow **Adding Mitered Borders**, page 151, to sew **borders** to center section to complete **Wall Hanging Top**.

COMPLETING THE WALL HANGING

1. Follow **Quilting**, page 151, to mark, layer, and quilt using **Quilting Diagram** as a suggestion. Our wall hanging is hand quilted.
2. Follow **Making a Hanging Sleeve**, page 157, to attach hanging sleeve to wall hanging.
3. Follow **Binding**, page 155, to bind wall hanging using 2 1/2"w straight-grain binding with mitered corners.

Quilting Diagram

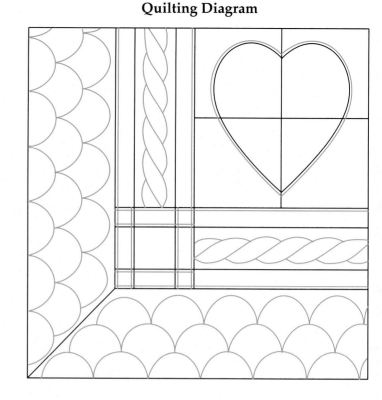

Wall Hanging Top Diagram

Heart

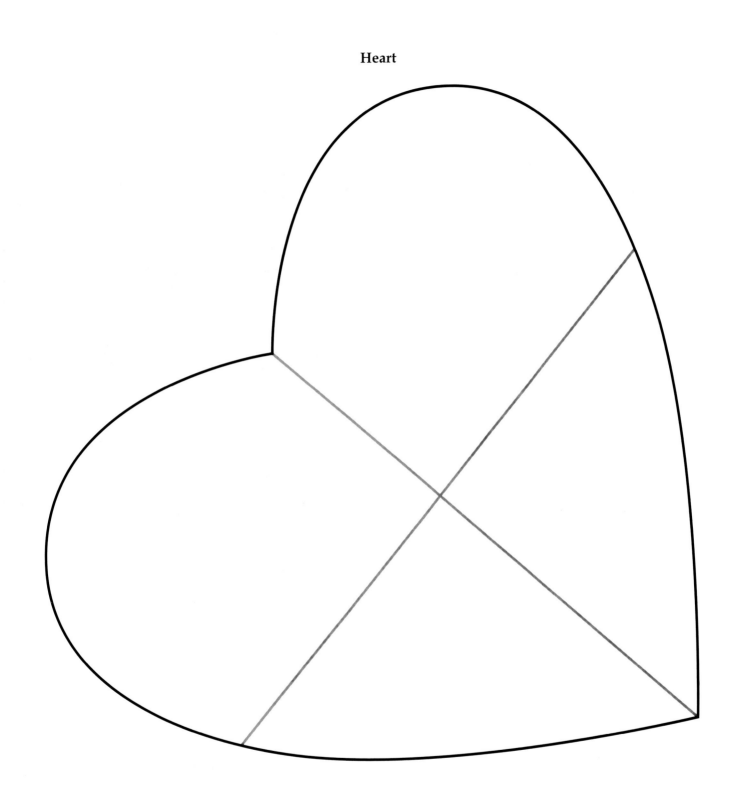

NURSERY RHYME CRIB SET

Hey, Diddle-Diddle, you'll adore the childhood charm of our nursery rhyme crib set! All the pieces are so easy to make, you'll laugh to see such sport. The cuddly collection includes a colorful quilt, bumper pads, and dust ruffle — all pieced with cheerful prints in shades of gold, blue and purple. The stars of the story, however, are the captivating cow motifs that leap over the moons on the quilt and bumper panel. Quick to fuse in place, the appliqués are stitched with clear nylon thread, so there's no need to change colors to match each fabric. A final touch is added to baby's crib with the simple dust ruffle that's edged with plain fabric strips.

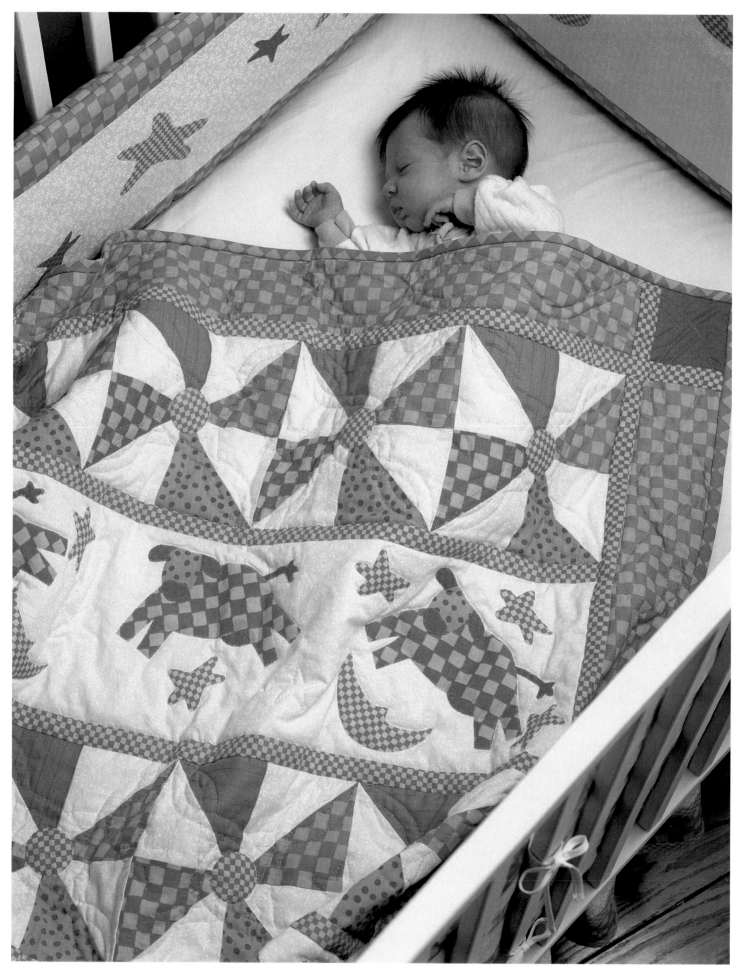

Nestled beneath the lovable motifs and patchwork blocks of our "a-moo-sing" comforter (opposite), baby will drift sweetly off to dreamland. The quilted chair pad (below), a star-crossed companion to our delightful crib set, will give Mom a touch of comfort, too. Each Pinwheel block is easy to make using four basic triangle-squares with a circle appliquéd over the center. For an extra-easy finish, the front and back layers of the pad are sewn together with batting and then turned right-side out for quilting. No binding is used for the edges, which makes the pad a real timesaver!

NURSERY RHYME CRIB QUILT

SKILL LEVEL: 1 2 3 4 5
BLOCK SIZE: 7¹/₂" x 7¹/₂"
QUILT SIZE: 38" x 49"

YARDAGE REQUIREMENTS
Yardage is based on 45"w fabric.

- 1¹/₂ yds of white print
- ⁷/₈ yd of blue check
- ⁵/₈ yd of gold check
- ³/₈ yd of blue dot
- ³/₈ yd of purple check
- ³/₈ yd of purple stripe
- ¹/₈ yd of pink check
  2⁵/₈ yds for backing
  ³/₄ yd for binding
  45" x 60" batting

You will also need:
  paper-backed fusible web
  transparent monofilament thread for appliqué

CUTTING OUT THE PIECES
All measurements include seam allowances. Follow Rotary Cutting, page 144, to cut fabric.

1. **From white print:**
   - Cut 4 **rectangles** 11" x 15" for triangle-squares.
   - Cut 2 **panels** 9" x 31¹/₂".

2. **From blue check:**
   - Cut 2 **side outer borders** 3¹/₂" x 41".
   - Cut 2 **top/bottom outer borders** 3¹/₂" x 30¹/₂".
   - Cut 1 **rectangle** 11" x 15" for triangle-squares.

3. **From gold check:**
   - Cut 2 **side inner borders** 1¹/₄" x 41".
   - Cut 2 **top/bottom inner borders** 1¹/₄" x 38".
   - Cut 4 **sashing strips** 1¹/₄" x 30¹/₂".
   - Cut 4 **sashing pieces** 1¹/₄" x 3¹/₂".

4. **From blue dot:**
   - Cut 1 **rectangle** 11" x 15" for triangle-squares.

5. **From purple check:**
   - Cut 1 **rectangle** 11" x 15" for triangle-squares.

6. **From purple stripe:**
   - Cut 1 **rectangle** 11" x 15" for triangle-squares.

7. **From pink check:**
   - Cut 4 **corner squares** 3¹/₂" x 3¹/₂".

PREPARING THE APPLIQUÉS
Follow Preparing Fusible Appliqués, page 149, to cut appliqués using patterns, page 85.

1. **From purple check:**
   - Cut 6 **bodies**.

2. **From pink check:**
   - Cut 6 **tails**.
   - Cut 6 **udders**.
   - Cut 6 **noses**.
   - Cut 12 **ears** (6 in reverse).

3. **From blue dot:**
   - Cut 6 **heads**.

4. **From gold check:**
   - Cut 12 **circles**.
   - Cut 4 **moons**.
   - Cut 14 **small stars**.

ASSEMBLING THE QUILT TOP
Follow Piecing and Pressing, page 146, to make quilt top.

1. To make triangle-squares, place 1 white print and blue check **rectangle** right sides together. Referring to **Fig. 1**, follow **Making Triangle-Squares**, page 147, to complete 12 **triangle-squares**. Repeat with remaining **rectangles** to make a total of 48 **triangle-squares** (12 from each color combination).

Fig. 1

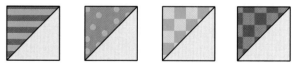

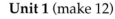

triangle-squares (make 12 of each)

2. Sew 4 **triangle-squares** together to make **Unit 1**. Make 12 **Unit 1's**.

Unit 1 (make 12)

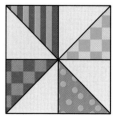

3. Follow **Invisible Appliqué**, page 150, to stitch 1 **circle** to the center of each **Unit 1** to make **Block**. Make 12 **Blocks**.

Block (make 12)

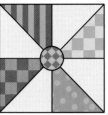

4. Placing appliqués at least 1" from outer edges of panel, follow **Invisible Appliqué**, page 150, to stitch **appliqués** to **panel**. Trim **panel** to 8" x 30½" to complete **Appliquéd Panel**. Make 2 **Appliquéd Panels**.

Appliquéd Panel (make 2)

5. Sew 4 **Blocks** together to make **Row**. Make 3 **Rows**.

Row (make 3)

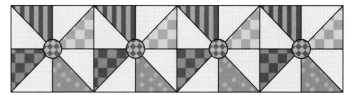

6. Referring to **Quilt Top Diagram**, page 80, sew **Rows**, **Appliquéd Panels**, and **sashing strips** together to make center section of quilt top.
7. Sew **side inner borders**, then **side outer borders** to sides of center section.
8. Sew **top/bottom inner borders** to center section.
9. Sew 2 **corner squares**, 2 **sashing pieces**, and 1 **top/bottom outer border** together to make **Border Unit**. Make 2 **Border Units**.

Border Unit (make 2)

10. Sew **Border Units** to top and bottom of center section to complete **Quilt Top**.

COMPLETING THE QUILT

1. Follow **Quilting**, page 151, to mark, layer, and quilt using **Quilting Diagram** as a suggestion. Our quilt is hand quilted.
2. Cut a 22" square of binding fabric. Follow **Binding**, page 155, to bind quilt using 2½"w bias binding with mitered corners.

Quilting Diagram

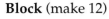

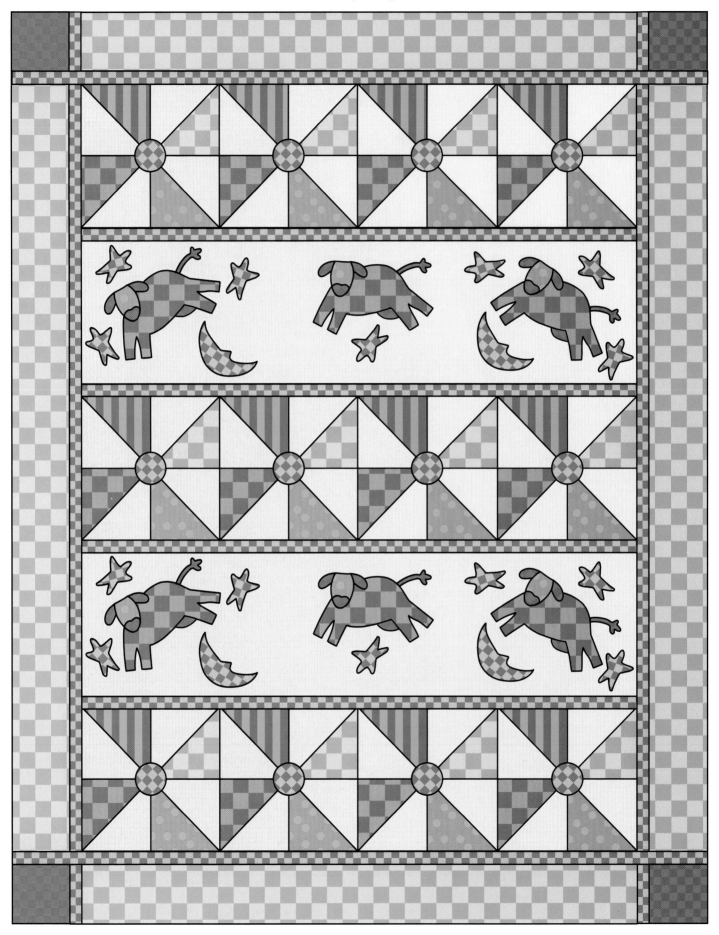

DUST RUFFLE

DUST RUFFLE LENGTH: 11"

YARDAGE REQUIREMENTS
Yardage is based on 45"w fabric.

☐ 2³/₈ yds of white print
▦ 1 yd of gold check
▦ ⁷/₈ yd of blue check
1⁵/₈ yds of white solid for deck

CUTTING OUT THE PIECES
Follow Rotary Cutting, page 144, to cut the following pieces, piecing as necessary to obtain indicated lengths.

1. From white print, cut 2 **side pieces** 8¹/₄" x 126" and 2 **head/foot pieces** 8¹/₄" x 69".
2. From gold check, cut 2 **side pieces** 1¹/₄" x 126", 2 **side pieces** 1¹/₂" x 126", 2 **head/foot pieces** 1¹/₄" x 69", and 2 **head/foot pieces** 1¹/₂" x 69".
3. From blue check, cut 2 **side pieces** 2¹/₂" x 126" and 2 **head/foot pieces** 2¹/₂" x 69".
4. From white solid, cut 1 **deck** 28" x 53".

MAKING THE DUST RUFFLE
Follow Piecing and Pressing, page 146, to make dust ruffle.

1. Placing 1¹/₂"w gold check **side piece** at bottom edge, sew **side pieces** together to make **Side Ruffle**. Make 2 **Side Ruffles**. Repeat with **head/foot pieces** to make 1 **Head** and 1 **Foot Ruffle**.

Ruffle

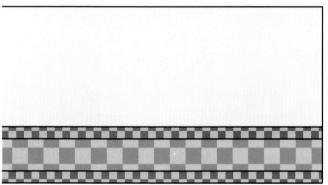

2. To finish bottom and side edges of each ruffle, press bottom edge ¹/₄" to wrong side; press ¹/₄" to wrong side again and stitch in place. Repeat for side edges.
3. To gather top edge of each **Ruffle**, baste ³/₈" and ¹/₄" from raw edge.
4. Beginning and ending ¹/₂" from each end of **deck**, pin top edge of 1 **Side Ruffle** to 1 long (side) edge of **deck**. Pull basting threads, drawing up gathers to fit edge of **deck**. Stitch **Side Ruffle** to deck using a ¹/₂" seam allowance.

5. Repeat Step 4 to sew remaining **Side Ruffle** to side edge and **Head** and **Foot Ruffles** to top and bottom edges of **deck** to complete **Dust Ruffle**.

PINWHEEL CHAIR PAD

BLOCK SIZE: 7¹/₂" x 7¹/₂"
CHAIR PAD SIZE: 13¹/₂" x 24¹/₂"

Our chair pad fits a rocking chair with a 14"w back. You may need to adjust the border size and placement of ties to fit your chair.

YARDAGE REQUIREMENTS
Yardage is based on 45"w fabric.

▦ ⁵/₈ yd of blue check
☐ ¹/₄ yd of white print
▦ ¹/₄ yd of gold check
◩ 6" x 6" square *each* of purple check, blue dot, and purple stripe
¹/₂ yd for backing
18" x 29" batting

You will also need:
paper-backed fusible web
transparent monofilament thread for appliqué

CUTTING OUT THE PIECES
All measurements include a ¹/₄" seam allowance. Follow Rotary Cutting, page 144, to cut fabric unless otherwise indicated.

1. **From blue check:** ▦
   - Cut 2 **side outer borders** 2³/₄" x 25".
   - Cut 2 **top/bottom outer borders** 2³/₄" x 9¹/₂".
   - Cut 2 **ties** 2¹/₂" x 32".
   - Cut 1 square 4⁵/₈" x 4⁵/₈". Cut square once diagonally to make 2 **triangles**.

2. **From white print:** ☐
   - Cut 1 **rectangle** 2¹/₂" x 8".
   - Cut 4 squares 4⁵/₈" x 4⁵/₈". Cut squares once diagonally to make 8 **triangles**.

3. **From gold check:** ▦
   - Cut 2 **side inner borders** 1¹/₄" x 19".
   - Cut 2 **top/bottom inner borders** 1¹/₄" x 9¹/₂".
   - Cut 2 **sashing strips** 1¹/₄" x 8".
   - Follow **Preparing Fusible Appliqués**, page 149, and use patterns, page 85, to cut 2 **circles** and 2 **small stars**.

4. **From purple check, blue dot, and purple stripe:** ◩
   - From *each* fabric, cut 1 square 4⁵/₈" x 4⁵/₈". Cut squares once diagonally to make 6 **triangles** (2 from each color).

ASSEMBLING THE CHAIR PAD TOP

Follow Piecing and Pressing, page 146, to make chair pad top.

1. Sew **triangles** together to make **triangle-squares**. Make a total of 8 **triangle-squares** (2 from each color combination).

triangle-squares (make 2 of each)

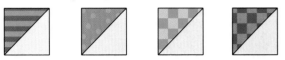

2. Follow Step 2 of **Assembling the Quilt Top**, page 78, to make 2 **Unit 1's**.
3. Referring to **Chair Pad Diagram**, sew **Unit 1's**, **sashing strips**, and **rectangle** together to make center section of chair pad top.
4. Follow **Invisible Appliqué**, page 150, to stitch 1 **circle** to the center of each **Unit 1** and 2 **small stars** to **rectangle**.
5. Sew **side**, then **top** and **bottom inner borders** to center section. Add **top**, **bottom**, then **side outer borders** to complete **Chair Pad Top**.

COMPLETING THE CHAIR PAD

1. Fold each **tie** in half lengthwise with right sides together. Sew raw edges together, leaving an opening for turning. Cut corners diagonally and turn right side out; press. Blindstitch openings closed.
2. Matching ends, fold each tie in half. Referring to **Chair Pad Diagram**, baste folded edges to top edge of chair pad top.
3. Cut backing and batting same size as chair pad top. Baste batting to wrong side of backing. With right sides together, sew backing and chair pad top together, leaving an opening at bottom edge for turning. Cut corners diagonally and turn right side out; blindstitch opening closed.
4. Follow **Quilting**, page 151, to mark and quilt using **Quilting Diagram** as a suggestion. Our chair pad is hand quilted.

Quilting Diagram

Chair Pad Diagram

BUMPER PADS

Our bumper pads fit a standard (27" x 52") baby bed.

YARDAGE REQUIREMENTS

Yardage is based on 45"w fabric.

☐ 3 yds of white print
▨ 2¹/₂ yds of blue check
▨ ¹/₂ yd of gold check
▨ ³/₈ yd of pink check
▨ ¹/₈ yd of purple check
▨ ¹/₈ yd of blue dot
   2¹/₄ yds of 72"w upholstery batting
   8 yds of ¹/₄"w white double-fold bias tape

You will also need:
   transparent monofilament thread for appliqué
   paper-backed fusible web
   19¹/₂" x 28" piece of paper (newsprint or craft paper)

CUTTING OUT THE PIECES

Follow Rotary Cutting, page 144, to cut the following pieces, piecing as necessary to obtain indicated lengths.

1. From white print, cut 4 **side panels** 8" x 53", 2 **foot panels** 8" x 28", and 2 **rectangles** 20" x 29".
2. From blue check, cut 8 **side strips** 2¹/₂" x 53", 4 **foot strips** 2¹/₂" x 28", 2 **head strips** 2¹/₂" x 28", and 2 **rectangles** 14" x 29".

PREPARING THE APPLIQUÉS

*Follow **Preparing Fusible Appliqués**, page 149, and use patterns, page 85, to cut the following **appliqués**.*

1. From purple check, cut 6 **bodies**.
2. From gold check, cut 26 **large stars**, 18 **small stars**, and 6 **moons**.
3. From pink check, cut 32 **small stars**, 6 **tails**, 6 **udders**, 6 **noses**, and 12 **ears** (6 in reverse).
4. From blue dot, cut 6 **heads**.

MAKING THE BUMPER PADS

*Follow **Piecing and Pressing**, page 146, to make bumper pads.*

1. To make head panel pattern, refer to **Fig. 1** to fold paper in half, matching short edges. Mark a point on short edge of paper 10" from bottom. Beginning at top of fold, draw a gentle freehand curve to marked point. Cut through both layers of paper and unfold.

Fig. 1

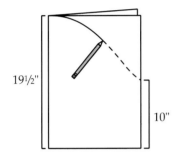

2. Use pattern to cut 2 **head panels** from white print **rectangles** and 2 batting pieces. Set batting aside for use in Step 8.
3. To make pattern for head panel trim, refer to **Fig. 2** to mark a line 2" from top edge of head panel pattern. Cut along marked line and discard lower portion.

Fig. 2

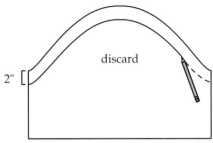

4. Use pattern to cut 2 **head panel trims** from blue check **rectangles**.
5. (*Note:* Refer to panel diagrams, this page and page 84, for Steps 5 - 7.) Press lower edge of each **head panel trim** ¼" to wrong side. Matching raw edges, baste wrong side of 1 **head panel trim** to right side of each **head panel** along top edge. Topstitch lower edge of head panel trim to head panel. Sew 1 **head strip** to bottom edge of each **head panel**.

Foot Panel (make 2)

Side Panel (make 4)

Head Panel (make 2)

6. Sew 1 **foot strip** each to top and bottom edges of each **foot panel**. Sew 1 **side strip** to top and bottom edges of each **side panel**.

7. Follow **Invisible Appliqué**, page 150, to stitch **appliqués** to each **panel**.

8. Cut 4 pieces of batting 12" x 53" and 2 pieces 12" x 28". Baste 1 piece of batting to wrong side of each corresponding **foot**, **side**, and **head panel**.

9. Sewing through all thicknesses, sew 1 **side panel** to each short edge of **foot panel** to make **Bumper Panel**. Make 2 **Bumper Panels**. Trim batting as close as possible to seamlines; trim 1/2" from lower edge of batting.

10. Cut 17 pieces of bias tape 16"l. Fold ends of each piece 1/4" to inside; stitch along long edges. Fold each piece in half to make **ties**.

11. Referring to **Fig. 3** (appliqués are not shown), mark each long edge of 1 **Bumper Panel** 26 1/2" from ends. Lightly draw a line between marks across width of panel. Baste folded ends of **ties** as shown, adjusting location of ties at marks to fit your bed if necessary.

12. Place **Bumper Panels** right sides together. Using a 1/2" seam allowance, sew pieces together along top and side edges. Trim corners and turn right side out. Turn bottom raw edges 3/8" to inside; topstitch bottom edges together close to edge.

13. Stitch across width of bumper panels (through all thicknesses) along lines marked in Step 11 and along seamlines indicated in **Fig. 3** to complete **Side/Foot Bumper**.

14. Referring to **Fig. 4**, baste 4 **ties** to side edges of 1 **head panel**; baste remaining **tie** to top edge of panel in desired location to fit your bed. Place **head panels** right sides together. Using a 1/2" seam allowance, sew pieces together along top and side edges. Trim 1/2" from lower edge of batting. Trim corners and turn right side out. Turn bottom raw edges of bumpers 3/8" to inside; topstitch bottom edges together close to edge to complete **Head Bumper**.

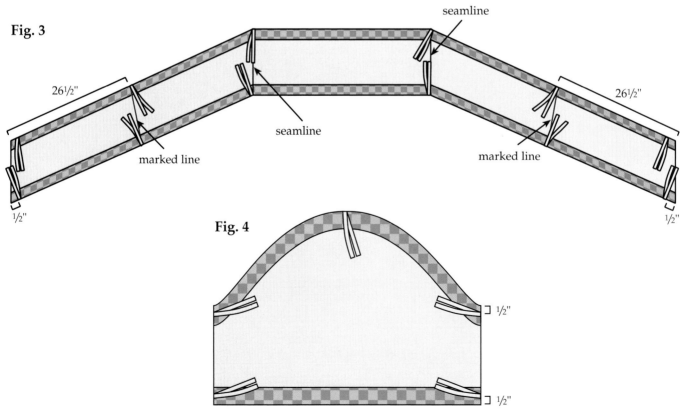

Fig. 3

26 1/2"   seamline   26 1/2"

seamline

marked line   marked line

1/2"   1/2"

Fig. 4

1/2"

1/2"

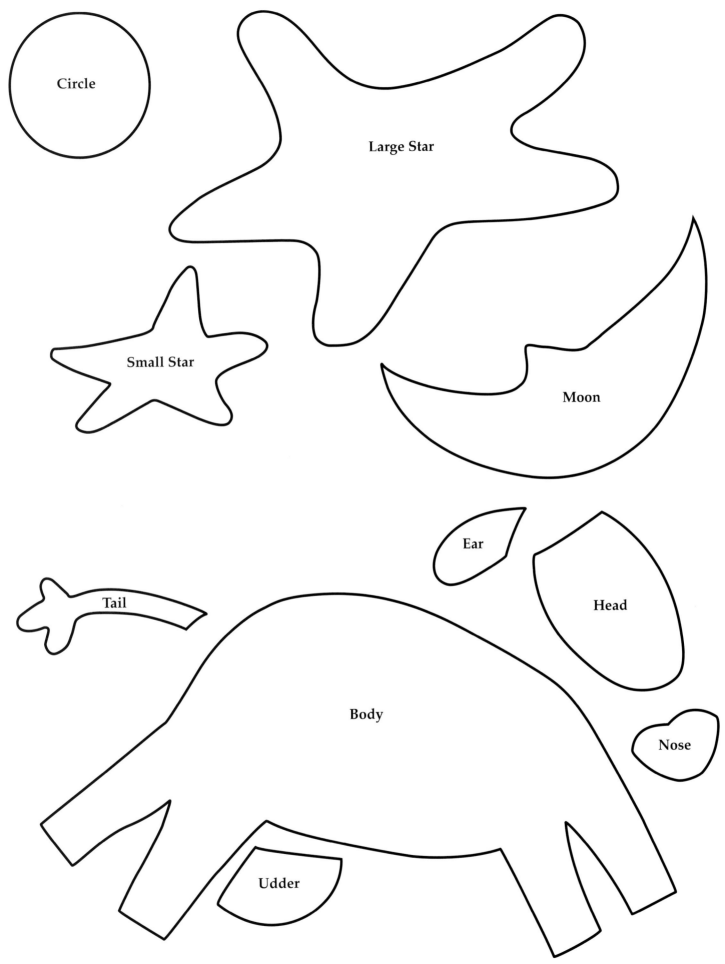

Circle

Large Star

Small Star

Moon

Ear

Head

Tail

Body

Nose

Udder

PINEAPPLE QUILT

Named for the symbol of hospitality that it resembles, the Pineapple pattern was a favorite of pioneer women. To help you re-create this vintage spread in a lot less time, we've simplified the construction using paper foundation piecing — a classic technique that has found a new following! The design is drawn onto tracing paper and then "punched" using an unthreaded sewing machine. This creates a perforated pattern for precise piecing and alignment of fabric strips as they're sewn together. We also added corner triangles to the octagon-shaped pieces to form square blocks for faster assembly of the rows and to eliminate set-in squares.

PINEAPPLE QUILT

SKILL LEVEL: 1 2 3 4 5
BLOCK SIZE: 15" x 15"
QUILT SIZE: 76" x 91"

Our antique quilt uses cream set-in squares to join the octagonal pineapple blocks. We simplified the construction of this quilt by adding corner triangles to make each block square. This eliminates the set-in squares and makes assembly of the quilt top much easier.

YARDAGE REQUIREMENTS

Yardage is based on 45"w fabric. Yardages given for quilt top fabrics are approximate.

- ☐ 7 yds of cream solid
- ■ $3^5/_8$ yds of red solid
- ▨ $3^3/_8$ yds of green solid
  $5^1/_2$ yds for backing
  $^7/_8$ yd for binding
  90" x 108" batting

You will also need:
   tracing paper (available at office supply stores in
      19" x 24" tablets)

CUTTING OUT THE PIECES

*Follow **Rotary Cutting**, page 144, to cut fabric. Due to variations in individual work and the nature of paper piecing, the actual number of strips needed may vary.*

1. **From cream solid:** ☐
   - Cut 90 **strips** $1^3/_4$"w.
   - Cut 10 strips 7"w. From these strips, cut 60 squares 7" x 7". Cut squares once diagonally to make 120 **corner triangles**.

2. **From red solid:** ■
   - Cut 60 **strips** $1^3/_4$"w.
   - Cut 2 strips $2^5/_8$"w. From these strips, cut 30 **center squares** $2^5/_8$" x $2^5/_8$".

3. **From green solid:** ▨
   - Cut 60 **strips** $1^3/_4$"w.

MAKING THE PAPER FOUNDATIONS

1. To make a full-size foundation pattern from pattern, page 91, use a ruler to draw a line down the center of a piece of tracing paper. Turn paper 90° and draw a second line down the center perpendicular to the first line. Place paper over pattern, matching grey lines of pattern to intersecting lines on paper. Trace pattern. Turn paper and trace pattern in each remaining corner. Do not cut out.

2. To make foundations, stack up to 12 sheets of paper together and pin pattern on top, being careful not to pin over traced lines. Use an unthreaded sewing machine with stitch length set at approximately 8 stitches per inch to "sew"

over traced lines of pattern, perforating the paper through all layers. These perforated lines will be your sewing lines. Trim foundations to approximately $^1/_4$" from outer line. Refer to **Block Diagram** and transfer corresponding numbers to each foundation. Repeat to make a total of 30 **foundations**.

ASSEMBLING THE QUILT TOP

1. (*Note:* Refer to **Block Diagram** for color placement. Numbers are not shown on **Figs. 1 - 4**.) Place 1 **center square** right side up over center square area on numbered side of 1 **foundation**; pin in place (**Fig. 1**). Hold foundation up to a light to make sure enough fabric extends beyond the center square outline (sewing line) for seam allowance.

Fig. 1

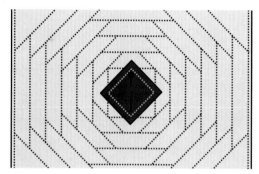

2. To cover area 1 on foundation, refer to **Fig. 2** to place 1 cream **strip** wrong side up on **center square**. Turn foundation over to paper side and sew directly on top of sewing line between center square and area 1, extending stitching a few stitches beyond beginning and end of line. Turn over to fabric side (**Fig. 2**).

Fig. 2

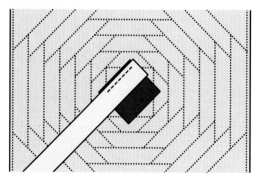

3. Trim strip even with ends of stitching. Trim seam allowance to a scant $^1/_4$" if necessary (**Fig. 3**). Open out strip and trim off corners, making sure enough fabric extends beyond adjacent seamlines for seam allowance. Press and pin strip to foundation.

Fig. 3

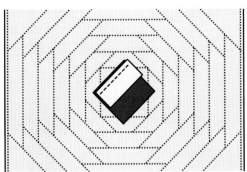

4. Repeat Steps 2 and 3 for areas 2, 3, and 4 (**Fig 4**).

Fig. 4

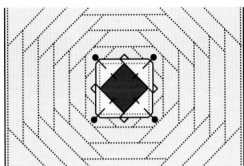

5. Referring to **Block Diagram**, repeat Steps 2 and 3 to add **strips** for areas 5 - 48 and to add **corner triangles** for areas 49 - 52 in numerical order. Trim block ¼" from outer line of block outline on **foundation** to complete **Block**. Make 30 **Blocks**.

Block (make 30)

6. Sew 5 **Blocks** together to make **Row**. Make 6 **Rows**.

Row (make 6)

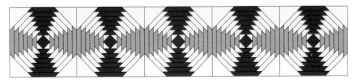

7. Referring to **Quilt Top Diagram**, page 90, sew **Rows** together. Carefully tear away **foundations** to complete **Quilt Top**.

COMPLETING THE QUILT

1. Follow **Quilting**, page 151, to mark, layer, and quilt using **Quilting Diagram** as a suggestion. Our quilt is hand quilted.
2. Cut a 30" square of binding fabric. Follow **Binding**, page 155, to bind quilt using 2½"w bias binding with mitered corners.

Block Diagram

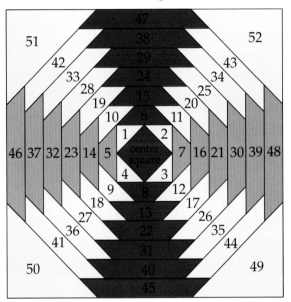

Quilting Diagram

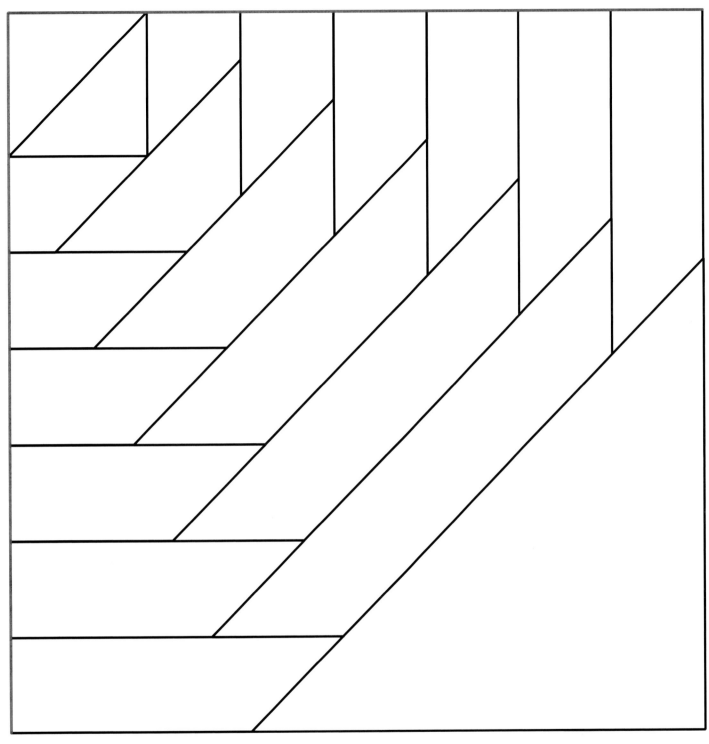

LITTLE QUILTS

Sure to be found among a pioneer
girl's playthings was at least one tiny
doll quilt, which provided loving warmth
for a family of rag dolls. The miniature work
might have been pieced as a sampler by a
grandmother, or it may even have been the
canvas for a girl's first unrefined stitches.
The small size of such quilts makes them
ideal projects for today's busy quilters.
And these little treasures don't have to be
limited to make-believe — use them for
delightful decorative accents, too! Our
LeMoyne Star wall hanging duplicates
an old-fashioned look with a traditional
pattern pieced in double-pink and brown
calicoes. Rotary-cut diamonds and simple
borders make it child's play to complete.

When not used for snuggling teddy bears, these miniature pieces can add a playful touch to your decor. Simply follow our general instructions to attach a hanging sleeve to the Delectable Mountains doll quilt (below) or the Charm doll quilt (opposite) to create a sweet wall hanging. Instructions for making the Delectable Mountains doll quilt can be found on page 15.

LeMOYNE STAR WALL HANGING

SKILL LEVEL: 1 2 3 4 5
BLOCK SIZE: 6" x 6"
WALL HANGING SIZE: 23" x 23"

YARDAGE REQUIREMENTS
Yardage is based on 45"w fabric.

- ☐ 3/8 yd of cream solid
- ▨ 1/4 yd of pink print for outer borders
- ■ 1/8 yd of brown print
- ◣ 1/8 yd *each* of 4 light pink prints and 2 dark pink prints
- 3/4 yd for backing and hanging sleeve
- 3/8 yd for binding
- 27" x 27" batting

CUTTING OUT THE PIECES
All measurements include a 1/4" seam allowance. Follow Rotary Cutting, page 144, to cut fabric.

1. **From cream solid:** ☐
   - Cut 2 strips 2¼"w. From these strips, cut 36 **squares** 2¼" x 2¼".
   - Cut 1 strip 3¾"w. From this strip, cut 9 squares 3¾" x 3¾". Cut squares twice diagonally to make 36 **triangles**.

2. **From pink print for outer borders:** ▨
   - Cut 2 **side outer borders** 1¾" x 20".
   - Cut 2 **top/bottom outer borders** 1¾" x 22½".

3. **From brown print:** ■
   - Cut 2 **side inner borders** 1¼" x 18½".
   - Cut 2 **top/bottom inner borders** 1¼" x 20".

4. **From 4 light and 2 dark pink prints:** ◣
   - Cut 1 **strip** 1¾"w from *each* light pink print.
   - Cut 2 **strips** 1¾"w from *each* dark pink print.

ASSEMBLING THE WALL HANGING TOP
Follow Piecing and Pressing, page 146, to make wall hanging top.

1. Referring to **Fig. 1**, align 45° marking on ruler (shown in pink) along lower edge of 1 light pink **strip**. Cut along right edge of ruler to cut 1 end of **strip** at a 45° angle. Repeat for remaining light and dark pink **strips**.

Fig. 1

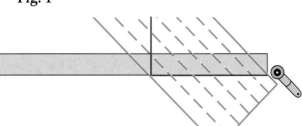

2. Turn 1 cut **strip** 180° on mat and align 45° marking on ruler along lower edge of **strip**. Align previously cut 45° edge with 1¾" marking on ruler. Cut **strips** at 1¾" intervals as shown in **Fig. 2**. Cut 9 **diamonds** from each **strip** (you will need a total of 36 light pink **diamonds** and 36 dark pink **diamonds**).

Fig. 2

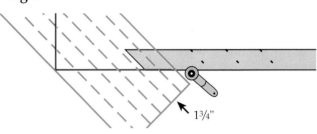

1¾"

3. Follow **Working with Diamond Shapes**, page 148, to sew 4 different light pink **diamonds**, 2 different pairs of dark pink **diamonds**, 4 **triangles**, and 4 **squares** together to make **Block**. Make 9 **Blocks**.

Block (make 9)

4. Referring to **Wall Hanging Top Diagram**, sew **Blocks** together to make center section of wall hanging top.

5. Sew **side**, then **top** and **bottom inner borders** to center section. Repeat to add **outer borders** to complete **Wall Hanging Top**.

COMPLETING THE WALL HANGING

1. Follow **Quilting**, page 151, to mark, layer, and quilt. Our wall hanging is hand quilted with lines radiating from the center of each star and in the ditch around borders.

2. Follow **Making a Hanging Sleeve**, page 157, and **Binding**, page 155, to complete wall hanging using 2½"w straight-grain binding with overlapped corners.

Wall Hanging Top Diagram

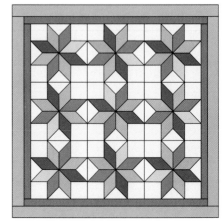

CHARM DOLL QUILT

SKILL LEVEL: 1 2 3 4 5
BLOCK SIZE: 6¹/₂" x 6¹/₂"
QUILT SIZE: 24" x 30"

YARDAGE REQUIREMENTS

Yardage is based on 45"w fabric.

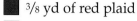 ³/₈ yd of red plaid

scraps of 48 different light prints

scraps of 48 different dark prints
⁷/₈ yd for backing
⁵/₈ yd for binding
28" x 34" batting

You will also need:
Easy Angle™ Rotary Cutting Ruler (made by EZ International)

CUTTING OUT THE PIECES

All measurements include a ¹/₄" seam allowance. Follow Rotary Cutting, page 144, to cut fabric.

1. **From red plaid:**
   • Cut 2 **side borders** 2" x 26¹/₂".
   • Cut 2 **top/bottom borders** 2" x 23".

2. **From scraps of light and dark prints:**
   • Follow **Cutting Out the Triangles**, page 128, to cut 48 **light triangles** and 48 **dark triangles**.

ASSEMBLING THE QUILT TOP

Follow Piecing and Pressing, page 146, to make quilt top.

1. Sew 1 **dark** and 1 **light triangle** together to make **triangle-square**. Make 48 **triangle-squares**.

triangle-square (make 48)

2. Sew 4 **triangle-squares** together to make **Block**. Make 12 **Blocks**.

Block (make 12)

3. Sew 3 **Blocks** together to make **Row**. Make 4 **Rows**.

Row (make 4)

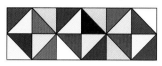

4. Referring to **Quilt Top Diagram**, sew **Rows** together to make center section of quilt top.
5. Sew **side**, then **top** and **bottom borders** to center section to complete **Quilt Top**.

COMPLETING THE QUILT

1. Follow **Quilting**, page 151, to mark, layer, and quilt using **Quilting Diagram** as a suggestion. Our quilt is hand quilted.
2. Cut a 19" square of binding fabric. Follow **Binding**, page 155, to bind quilt using 2¹/₂"w bias binding with mitered corners.

Quilt Top Diagram

Quilting Diagram

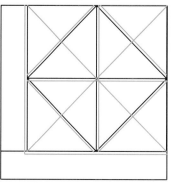

FLORAL NINE-PATCH

Even a pattern as basic as the Nine-Patch can blossom into a contemporary beauty when pieced with daringly coordinated fabrics. It's fun to mix and match a variety of prints and watch the drama unfold! For our Floral Nine-Patch quilt, we selected a bold floral print and accented it with several smaller prints in complementary shades. The similar color values that result create a visually striking arrangement within the easy-to-piece blocks. Offset with simple strip-set sashing and plain setting squares, the blocks are enhanced with wide floral and green print borders.

FLORAL NINE-PATCH QUILT

SKILL LEVEL: 1 2 3 4 5
BLOCK SIZE: 9" x 9"
QUILT SIZE: 86" x 98"

YARDAGE REQUIREMENTS
Yardage is based on 45"w fabric.

 4³/₈ yds of large floral print

3³/₄ yds of green print

3⁵/₈ yds of purple print

1⁷/₈ yds of white print
8 yds for backing
1 yd for binding
120" x 120" batting

CUTTING OUT THE PIECES
All measurements include a ¹/₄" seam allowance. Follow **Rotary Cutting**, *page 144, to cut fabric.*

1. **From large floral print:**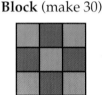
    - Cut 13 **wide strips** 3¹/₂"w.
    - Cut 4 strips 3¹/₂"w. From these strips, cut 42 **sashing squares** 3¹/₂" x 3¹/₂".
    - Cut 2 lengthwise **top/bottom wide borders** 8¹/₂" x 85".
    - Cut 2 lengthwise **side wide borders** 8¹/₂" x 81".

2. **From green print:**
    - Cut 18 **narrow strips** 1¹/₂"w.
    - Cut 2 lengthwise **side outer borders** 2¹/₂" x 97".
    - Cut 2 lengthwise **top/bottom outer borders** 2¹/₂" x 89".

3. **From purple print:**
    - Cut 11 **wide strips** 3¹/₂"w.
    - Cut 2 lengthwise **side inner borders** 1¹/₂" x 79".
    - Cut 2 lengthwise **top/bottom inner borders** 1¹/₂" x 69".

4. **From white print:**
    - Cut 36 **narrow strips** 1¹/₂"w.

ASSEMBLING THE QUILT TOP
Follow **Piecing and Pressing**, *page 146, to make quilt top.*

1. Sew 3 **wide strips** together to make **Strip Set A**. Make 5 **Strip Set A's**. Cut across **Strip Set A's** at 3¹/₂" intervals to make 60 **Unit 1's**.

Strip Set A (make 5)   **Unit 1** (make 60)

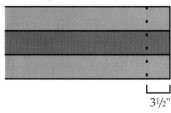

3¹/₂"

2. Sew 3 **wide strips** together to make **Strip Set B**. Make 3 **Strip Set B's**. Cut across **Strip Set B's** at 3¹/₂" intervals to make 30 **Unit 2's**.

Strip Set B (make 3)   **Unit 2** (make 30)

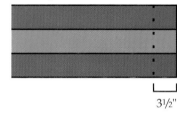

3¹/₂"

3. Sew 2 **Unit 1's** and 1 **Unit 2** together to make **Block**. Make 30 **Blocks**.

Block (make 30)

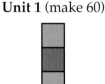

4. Sew 3 **narrow strips** together to make **Strip Set C**. Make 18 **Strip Set C's**. Cut across **Strip Set C's** at 9¹/₂" intervals to make 71 **Sashing Units**.

Strip Set C (make 18)   **Sashing Unit** (make 71)

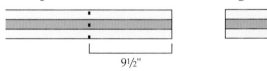

9¹/₂"

5. Sew 5 **Blocks** and 6 **Sashing Units** together to make **Row**. Make 6 **Rows**.

Row (make 6)

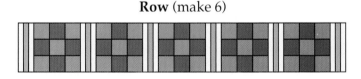

6. Sew 6 **sashing squares** and 5 **Sashing Units** together to make **Sashing Row**. Make 7 **Sashing Rows**.

Sashing Row (make 7)

7. Referring to **Quilt Top Diagram**, sew **Sashing Rows** and **Rows** together to make center section of quilt top.

8. Follow **Adding Squared Borders**, page 150, to sew **side**, then **top** and **bottom inner borders** to center section. Repeat to add **wide borders**, then **outer borders** to complete **Quilt Top**.

COMPLETING THE QUILT

1. Follow **Quilting**, page 151, to mark, layer, and quilt using **Quilting Diagram** as a suggestion. Our quilt is hand quilted.
2. Cut a 33" square of binding fabric. Follow **Binding**, page 155, to bind quilt using 2¹/₂"w bias binding with mitered corners.

Quilting Diagram

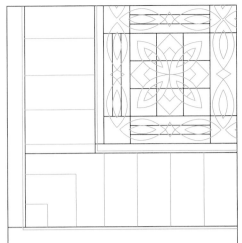

Quilt Top Diagram

HAUNTING COLLECTION

As fall arrives at your doorstep with a gust of vibrantly colored leaves, it's time to start decorating your home for a bewitching Halloween. A few handmade touches from our easy-to-make assortment can help you create hauntingly fun decor. Fashioned in a flash, the spirited wall hanging features spooky fused-on fabric cutouts. The playful design is especially fast because it's sewn with simple running stitches right onto the batting — with no backing or binding! Fabric letters are fused onto painted wooden blocks to spell out a greeting for your favorite goblins, and an adorable machine-sewn witch flies above a decorated clay flowerpot. Arranged with dried or silk foliage and fresh pumpkins, this madcap collection is ideal for celebrating All Hallows' Eve!

SPOOKY WALL HANGING

SKILL LEVEL: 1 2 3 4 5
WALL HANGING SIZE: 22" x 23"

SUPPLIES

1/4 yd of 45"w fabric for borders and hanging loops
20" x 21 1/2" fabric for background
scraps of assorted fabrics for appliqués
scrap of leaf print fabric for vine appliqués
22" x 23 1/2" cotton batting
paper-backed fusible web
embroidery floss
black permanent fabric marker

MAKING THE WALL HANGING

Patterns are shown on pages 104 - 107. Refer to patterns and photo when making wall hanging.

1. Follow manufacturer's instructions to fuse web to wrong side of border fabric. Cut 2 side borders 3/4" x 20", 2 top/bottom borders 3/4" x 21 1/2", and 4 hanging loop strips 3/4" x 7 1/2". Remove paper backing.

2. Fuse side, then top and bottom borders to background fabric 1/2" from outer edges.

3. Use patterns and follow **Preparing Fusible Appliqués**, page 149, to cut out 2 trees, 3 ghosts (1 in reverse), 1 moon, pieces for 1 house, pieces for 1 sign, pieces for 2 fences, and letters to spell out "TRICK OR TREAT." Cut a wavy shape for ground approximately 1 1/2" x 18 1/2". Cut leaves for vine from leaf print fabric.

4. Use fabric marker to add details to ghosts and windows (shown in blue on patterns) and to write "Ghost Crossing" on sign.

5. Arrange appliqués on background (tree shapes are overlapped). Fuse in place.

6. Center background on batting. Use 6 strands of floss and long running stitches to sew pieces together along edges of background.

7. Use your fingers to pick off small pieces along edges of batting to give batting a frayed look.

8. To make each hanging loop, fuse 2 hanging loop strips wrong sides together. Press ends under 1/4". Blindstitch pressed ends of hanging loops to front, then back of wall hanging.

WANDA WITCH

SUPPLIES

2 pieces of black fabric 9" x 11"
1 piece of orange check fabric 5" x 14"
1 piece of blue check fabric 3" x 3 3/4"
scraps of brown solid and cream solid fabrics
2 pieces of black felt 2" x 4"
12" of 3/8"w black satin ribbon
lightweight fusible interfacing
paper-backed fusible web
2 black 1/2" buttons
3 1/2" clay pot
floral foam
natural and green raffia
1 1/2" papier mâché pumpkin
11 1/2" of 3/16" dia. dowel
6" of 1/8" dia. dowel
black acrylic paint
small foam paintbrush
hot glue gun and glue sticks
black permanent fabric marker
peach colored pencil
tracing paper
polyester fiberfill

MAKING THE WITCH

Patterns are shown on page 107. Refer to patterns and photo when making witch.

1. For stuffed witch shape, trace outermost line of witch pattern onto tracing paper; cut out. Place black fabric pieces right sides together with pattern on top. Use a fabric marking pencil to draw around pattern. Sew pieces together directly on drawn line, leaving an opening for turning where indicated. Cut out 1/4" from stitching line, clipping curves and corners. Turn right side out and press.

2. From orange check fabric, cut 1 strip 3/4" x 14" for skirt trim, 1 strip 3/4" x 10" for hat trim, and 1 strip to fit around rim of pot.

3. Fuse interfacing to remaining orange check fabric and to cream solid and brown solid scraps.

4. Spacing patterns at least 1/2" apart, trace patterns A - F onto paper side of web. Cut patterns apart. Fuse patterns to wrong side of interfaced fabrics as follows: A - C to orange check, D and E to brown solid, and F to cream solid. Cut out pieces.

5. Use fabric marker to draw face details and peach pencil to color cheeks.

6. Remove paper backing from cutouts. Place witch with skirt facing to right. Fuse cutouts to witch.

Tree

7. Stuff witch with fiberfill; blindstitch opening closed.
8. For boots, use web to fuse felt pieces together. Trace boot pattern onto tracing paper; cut out. Use pattern to cut 2 boots from felt. Glue top 1/2" of boots to front of witch.
9. For hat trim, hand baste 1/8" from 1 long edge of hat trim strip. Pull thread, drawing up gathers so that gathered edge fits around hat 1 1/2" from top; knot thread. Glue in place.
10. Repeat Step 9 for skirt trim, gluing gathered edge around witch 3/4" from bottom of skirt and covering tops of boots.
11. For cape, hand baste 1/8" from 1 short edge of blue check fabric. Pull thread, gathering edge to 3/4"; knot thread. Glue cape to witch.
12. For bow, tie ribbon into a bow; trim ends. Glue bow to hat.
13. For hair, glue 1 1/2" lengths of green raffia around face.
14. For broom, fold several 4" lengths of natural raffia in half. Place folded ends around 1/8" dia. dowel 4" from top end. Knot a length of thread tightly around folded ends to secure. Tie a 6" length of natural raffia around broom, covering thread.
15. Glue broom to witch. Use black marker to darken dowel where buttons will be glued; glue buttons to broomstick.
16. Paint pot black using foam brush.
17. Glue pot trim strip around rim of pot.
18. Fill pot with floral foam to within 1/2" of top. Glue green and natural raffia in pot, covering foam. Glue pumpkin in pot.
19. Use seam ripper to remove 2 or 3 stitches from bottom of witch where indicated on pattern. Insert 3/16" dowel into witch. Insert dowel into foam; glue to secure.

"TRICK-OR-TREAT" BLOCKS

SUPPLIES
1 dozen 1 1/2" wooden blocks
black spray paint
scraps of assorted fabrics for appliqués
paper-backed fusible web

MAKING THE BLOCKS
1. Spray paint blocks; allow to dry.
2. Use patterns, page 106, and follow **Preparing Fusible Appliqués**, page 149, to cut out letters to spell "TRICK OR TREAT."
3. Fuse appliqués to blocks.

Moon

105

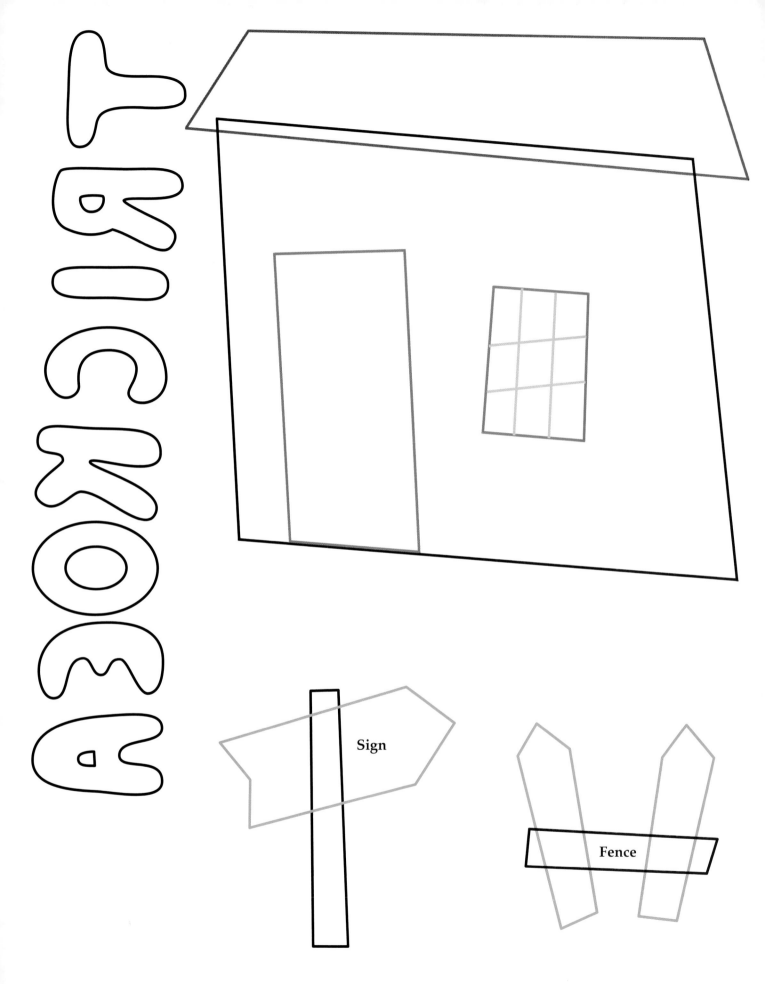

Sign

Fence

HICKORY

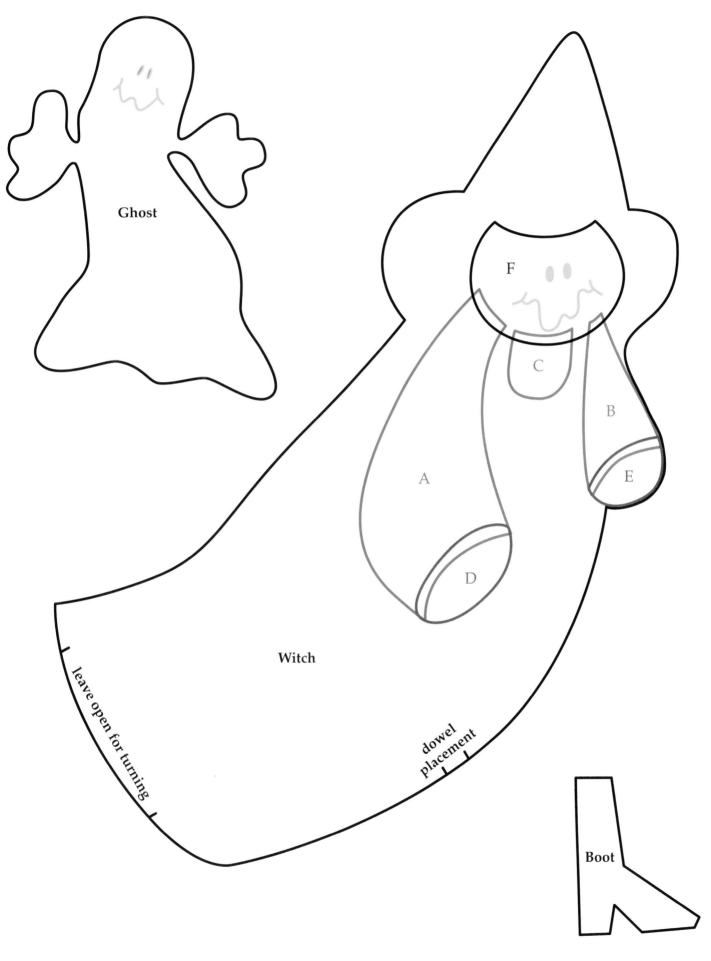

Ghost

Witch

leave open for turning

dowel placement

A

B

C

D

E

F

Boot

107

BACHELOR'S PUZZLE COLLECTION

One of the most notable milestones in the life of a young man in Early America was his advent into adulthood. At this time he would traditionally receive new apparel, known as his "Freedom Suit," and a grand "Freedom Quilt" pieced for the occasion by his mother, other female relatives, or even his sweetheart. The quiltmakers often represented the theme with a patriotic color scheme and manly quilt pattern, such as our Bachelor's Puzzle design. Featuring a handsome arrangement of geometric shapes, each block is actually very simple to construct using strip-pieced Nine-Patch units and grid-pieced triangle-squares. Easy strip-pieced sashing and Nine-Patch setting squares accentuate the overall design.

108

For a versatile accent, try this simple-to-make wall hanging — it's reversible! All-American red, white, and blue fabrics are used to create the four bold blocks on the front. Flip it over to reveal an oversize Bachelor's Puzzle block on the back, bordered with strip-pieced sashing and Nine-Patch setting squares. Finished with basic grid quilting, it will add a touch of tradition to a provincial den.

BACHELOR'S PUZZLE QUILT

SKILL LEVEL: 1 2 3 4 5
BLOCK SIZE: 15" x 15"
QUILT SIZE: 70" x 88"

The quilter who made our antique quilt arranged the nine-patch units randomly from block to block. To simplify construction, our instructions make placement of these units uniform throughout the quilt.

YARDAGE REQUIREMENTS

Yardage is based on 45"w fabric.

- ⬜ 4 yds of cream solid
- ⬛ 3³/₈ yds of red solid
- ⬛ 3³/₈ yds of blue solid
  5³/₈ yds for backing
  1 yd for binding
  81" x 96" batting

CUTTING OUT THE PIECES

*All measurements include a ¹/₄" seam allowance. Follow **Rotary Cutting**, page 144, to cut fabric.*

1. **From cream solid:** ⬜
   - Cut 42 **narrow strips** 1¹/₂"w.
   - Cut 6 **rectangles** 17" x 21" for triangle-squares.

2. **From red solid:** ⬛
   - Cut 31 **narrow strips** 1¹/₂"w.
   - Cut 5 **wide strips** 3¹/₂"w.
   - Cut 3 **rectangles** 17" x 21" for triangle-squares.

3. **From blue solid:** ⬛
   - Cut 32 **narrow strips** 1¹/₂"w.
   - Cut 5 **wide strips** 3¹/₂"w.
   - Cut 3 **rectangles** 17" x 21" for triangle-squares.

ASSEMBLING THE QUILT TOP

*Follow **Piecing and Pressing**, page 146, to make quilt top.*

1. To make triangle-square A's, place 1 red and 1 cream **rectangle** right sides together. Referring to **Fig. 1**, follow **Making Triangle-Squares**, page 147, to make 40 **triangle-square A's**. Repeat with remaining red **rectangles** and 2 cream **rectangles** to make a total of 120 **triangle-square A's**. Use blue **rectangles** and remaining cream **rectangles** and repeat to make a total of 120 **triangle-square B's**.

Fig. 1

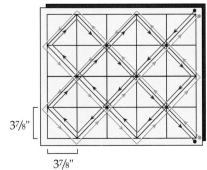

triangle-square A
(make 120)

triangle-square B
(make 120)

2. Sew 3 **narrow strips** together to make **Strip Set A**. Make 4 **Strip Set A's**. Cut across **Strip Set A's** at 1¹/₂" intervals to make 92 **Unit 1's**.

Strip Set A (make 4)   **Unit 1** (make 92)

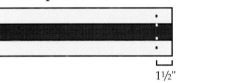

1½"

3. Sew 3 **narrow strips** together to make **Strip Set B**. Make 7 **Strip Set B's**. Cut across **Strip Set B's** at 1¹/₂" intervals to make 184 **Unit 2's**.

Strip Set B (make 7)   **Unit 2** (make 184)

1½"

4. Sew 1 **Unit 1** and 2 **Unit 2's** together to make **Unit 3**. Make 92 **Unit 3's**.

Unit 3 (make 92)

5. Sew **triangle-square A's**, **triangle-square B's**, and **Unit 3's** together to make 20 each of **Unit 4a**, **4b**, **4c**, and **4d**.

Unit 4a (make 20)   **Unit 4b** (make 20)

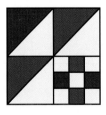   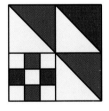

Unit 4c (make 20)   **Unit 4d** (make 20)

   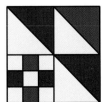

6. Sew 1 **wide** and 3 **narrow strips** together to make **Strip Set C**. Make 4 **Strip Set C's**. Cut across 2 **Strip Set C's** at 3½" intervals to make 20 **Unit 5's**.

Strip Set C (make 4)   **Unit 5** (make 20)

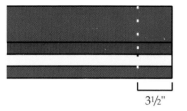

3½"

7. Sew 2 **Strip Set C's** and 1 **wide strip** together to make 1 **Strip Set D**. Cut across **Strip Set D** at 3½" intervals to make 10 **Unit 6's**.

Strip Set D (make 1)   **Unit 6** (make 10)

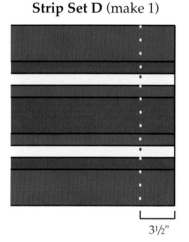
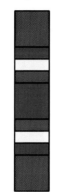

3½"

8. Sew 1 **wide** and 3 **narrow strips** together to make **Strip Set E**. Make 4 **Strip Set E's**. Cut across 2 **Strip Set E's** at 3½" intervals to make 20 **Unit 7's**.

Strip Set E (make 4)   **Unit 7** (make 20)

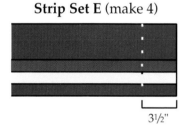

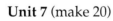

3½"

9. Sew 2 **Strip Set E's** and 1 **wide strip** together to make 1 **Strip Set F**. Cut across **Strip Set F** at 3½" intervals to make 10 **Unit 8's**.

Strip Set F (make 1)   **Unit 8** (make 10)

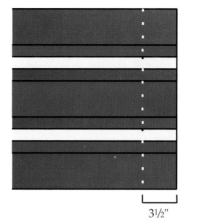

3½"

10. Sew 1 **Unit 4a**, 1 **Unit 5**, and 1 **Unit 4b** together to make **Unit 9**. Make 20 **Unit 9's**.

Unit 9 (make 20)

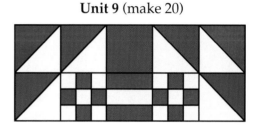

11. Sew 2 **Unit 9's** and 1 **Unit 6** together to make **Block A**. Make 10 **Block A's**.

Block A (make 10)

12. Sew 1 **Unit 4c**, 1 **Unit 7**, and 1 **Unit 4d** together to make **Unit 10**. Make 20 **Unit 10's**.

Unit 10 (make 20)

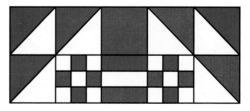

113

13. Sew 2 **Unit 10's** and 1 **Unit 8** together to make **Block B**. Make 10 **Block B's**.

Block B (make 10)

14. Sew 3 **narrow strips** together to make **Strip Set G**. Make 16 **Strip Set G's**. Cut across **Strip Set G's** at 15½" intervals to make 31 **Sashing Units**.

Strip Set G (make 16)   **Sashing Unit** (make 31)

15½"

15. Sew 2 **Block A's**, 2 **Block B's**, and 3 **Sashing Units** together to make **Row**. Make 5 **Rows**.

Row (make 5)

16. Sew 4 **Sashing Units** and 3 **Unit 3's** together to make **Sashing Row A**. Make 2 **Sashing Row A's**. Sew 4 **Sashing Units** and 3 **Unit 3's** together to make **Sashing Row B**. Make 2 **Sashing Row B's**.

Sashing Row A (make 2)

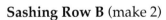

Sashing Row B (make 2)

17. Referring to **Quilt Top Diagram**, sew **Rows**, **Sashing Row A's**, and **Sashing Row B's** together to complete **Quilt Top**.

COMPLETING THE QUILT

1. Follow **Quilting**, page 151, to mark, layer, and quilt using **Quilting Diagram** as a suggestion. Our quilt is hand quilted.

2. Cut a 30" square of binding fabric. Follow **Binding**, page 155, to bind quilt using 2½"w bias binding with mitered corners.

Quilt Top Diagram

Quilting Diagram

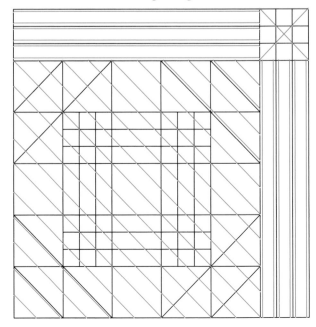

REVERSIBLE WALL HANGING

SKILL LEVEL: 1 2 3 4 5
WALL HANGING SIZE: 34" x 34"

YARDAGE REQUIREMENTS

Yardage is based on 45"w fabric.

☐ 2 yds of cream print

■ 1³/₄ yds of red print

■ 1⁷/₈ yds of blue print
   ³/₄ yd for binding and hanging loops
   38" x 38" batting

CUTTING OUT THE PIECES

All measurements include a ¹/₄" seam allowance. Follow
***Rotary Cutting**, page 144, to cut fabric.*

1. From cream print: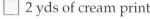
(for Wall Hanging Front)
- Cut 2 **rectangles** 13" x 17" for triangle-squares.
- Cut 10 **narrow strips** 1¹/₂"w. Cut 3 of these strips in half crosswise.

(for Wall Hanging Back)
- Cut 1 strip 5³/₈"w. From this strip, cut 6 squares 5³/₈" x 5³/₈". Cut squares once diagonally to make 12 **triangles**.
- Cut 2 **medium strips** 2"w. Cut strips in half crosswise.
- Cut 8 **border strips** 2¹/₄" x 23".

2. From red print: ■
(for Wall Hanging Front)
- Cut 1 **rectangle** 13" x 17" for triangle-squares.
- Cut 7 **narrow strips** 1¹/₂"w. Cut 3 of these strips in half crosswise.
- Cut 2 **wide strips** 3¹/₂"w. Cut strips in half crosswise.

(for Wall Hanging Back)
- Cut 2 squares 5³/₈" x 5³/₈". Cut each square once diagonally to make 4 **triangles**.
- Cut 1 **square** 5" x 5".
- Cut 1 **medium strip** 2"w. Cut strip in half crosswise.
- Cut 5 **border strips** 2¹/₄" x 23".

3. From blue print: ■
(for Wall Hanging Front)
- Cut 1 **rectangle** 13" x 17" for triangle-squares.
- Cut 7 **narrow strips** 1¹/₂"w. Cut 3 of these strips in half crosswise.
- Cut 2 **wide strips** 3¹/₂"w. Cut strips in half crosswise.

(for Wall Hanging Back)
- Cut 1 strip 5³/₈"w. From this strip, cut 4 squares 5³/₈" x 5³/₈". Cut squares once diagonally to make 8 **triangles**.
- Cut 4 **squares** 5" x 5".
- Cut 2 strips 2"w. Cut strips in half crosswise to make 4 **medium strips** (you will need 3 and have 1 left over).
- Cut 6 **border strips** 2¹/₄" x 23".

ASSEMBLING THE WALL HANGING

*Follow **Piecing and Pressing**, page 146, to make wall hanging front and back.*

WALL HANGING FRONT

1. To make triangle-square A's, place red and 1 cream **rectangle** right sides together. Referring to **Fig. 1**, follow **Making Triangle-Squares**, page 147, to make 24 **triangle-square A's**. Use blue and remaining cream **rectangle** and repeat to make 24 **triangle-square B's**.

Fig. 1

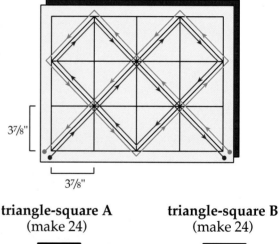

3⁷/₈"

3⁷/₈"

triangle-square A   triangle-square B
(make 24)   (make 24)

2. Referring to **Piecing Table**, page 116, for total number of Strip Sets, Units, Blocks, and Sashing Units needed, follow Steps 2 - 14 of **Assembling the Quilt Top**, page 112. When making **Strip Sets A**, **B**, and **G**, use full-length strips. When making **Strip Sets C**, **D**, **E**, and **F**, use strips that are cut in half.

Piecing Table

NAME	TOTAL NEEDED
Strip Set A	1
Unit 1	17
Strip Set B	2
Unit 2	34
Unit 3	17
Unit 4a	4
Unit 4b	4
Unit 4c	4
Unit 4d	4
Strip Set C	3
Unit 5	4
Strip Set D	1
Unit 6	2
Strip Set E	3
Unit 7	4
Strip Set F	1
Unit 8	2
Unit 9	4
Block A	2
Unit 10	4
Block B	2
Strip Set G	2
Sashing Unit	4

3. Sew **Block A's**, **Block B's**, **Unit 3**, and **Sashing Units** together to complete **Wall Hanging Front**.

Wall Hanging Front

WALL HANGING BACK

1. Sew 1 red and 1 cream **triangle** together to make **triangle-square A**. Make 4 **triangle-square A's**. Sew 1 blue and 1 cream **triangle** together to make **triangle-square B**. Make 8 **triangle-square B's**.

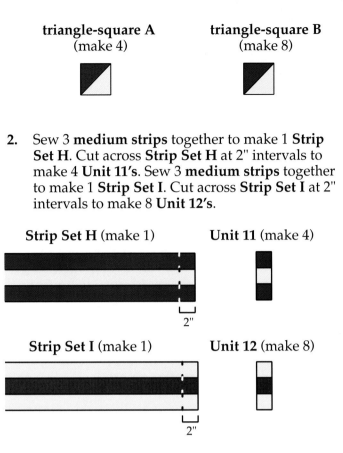

triangle-square A
(make 4)

triangle-square B
(make 8)

2. Sew 3 **medium strips** together to make 1 **Strip Set H**. Cut across **Strip Set H** at 2" intervals to make 4 **Unit 11's**. Sew 3 **medium strips** together to make 1 **Strip Set I**. Cut across **Strip Set I** at 2" intervals to make 8 **Unit 12's**.

Strip Set H (make 1)   **Unit 11** (make 4)

2"

Strip Set I (make 1)   **Unit 12** (make 8)

2"

3. Sew 1 **Unit 11** and 2 **Unit 12's** together to make **Unit 13**. Make 4 **Unit 13's**.

Unit 13 (make 4)

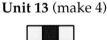

4. Sew **triangle-square A's**, **triangle-square B's**, and **Unit 13's** together to make 2 each of **Unit 14a** and **Unit 14b**.

Unit 14a (make 2)   **Unit 14b** (make 2)

5. Sew 3 **medium strips** together to make 1 **Strip Set J**. Cut across **Strip Set J** at 5" intervals to make 4 **Unit 15's**.

Strip Set J (make 1)   **Unit 15** (make 4)

 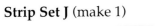

5"

Unit 15 (make 4)

6. Sew 1 **Unit 15** and 1 **square** together to make **Unit 16**. Make 4 **Unit 16's**.

Unit 16 (make 4)

7. Sew 2 **Unit 16's** and 1 **square** together to make 1 **Unit 17**.

Unit 17 (make 1)

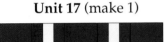

8. Sew 1 **Unit 14a**, 1 **Unit 16**, and 1 **Unit 14b** together to make **Unit 18**. Make 2 **Unit 18's**.

Unit 18 (make 2)

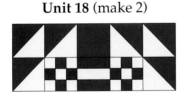

9. Sew 2 **Unit 18's** and 1 **Unit 17** together to make **Block**.

Block

10. Sew 3 **border strips** together to make **Border Unit**. Make 4 **Border Units**.

Border Unit (make 4)

11. Using remaining **border strips** and cutting across strip sets at 2¹/4" intervals, follow Steps 2 and 3 of **Wall Hanging Back**, page 116, to make 4 **Corner Squares**.

Corner Square (make 4)

12. Sew 1 **Border Unit** each to top and bottom edges of **Block**. Sew 1 **Corner Square** to each end of remaining **Border Units**. Sew **Border Units** to sides of **Block** to complete **Wall Hanging Back**.

Wall Hanging Back

COMPLETING THE WALL HANGING

1. Follow **Quilting**, page 151, to mark, layer, and quilt. Our wall hanging is hand quilted using a diagonal grid.
2. For hanging loops, cut 1 strip 5"w. Fold strip in half lengthwise with right sides together and sew along long raw edges to make tube. Turn right side out and press. Cut across tube at 6" intervals to make a total of 5 hanging loops. Matching raw edges, fold each hanging loop in half. Referring to photo and spacing loops evenly, baste raw edges of loops to top raw edge of wall hanging back.
3. Cut a 21" square of binding fabric. Follow **Binding**, page 155, to bind wall hanging using 2¹/2"w bias binding with mitered corners.

STARRY PATH

More than a hundred LeMoyne Stars create a colorful trail on our Starry Path quilt. This handsome spread is ideal for using up fabric scraps, or you can purchase fabrics in a wide assortment of colors and prints to achieve a similar look. Featuring eye-catching hand quilting, the large white setting blocks provide a cloud-soft atmosphere for the stars. A pieced border of diamonds and a dark blue binding finish the cozy coverlet. Precision rotary cutting offers stellar results on both the quilt and coordinating curtain tiebacks!

STARRY PATH QUILT

SKILL LEVEL: 1 2 3 4 5
STAR BLOCK SIZE: 6" x 6"
QUILT SIZE: 90" x 108"

Although our quilt was made using a variety of scrap fabrics for the stars, a similar scrappy look may be achieved by purchasing twenty-eight ¹/₄-yard cuts (not fat quarters) of assorted print fabrics.

YARDAGE REQUIREMENTS

Yardage is based on 45"w fabric.

☐ 7³/₄ yds of white solid

◼ 7 yds **total** of assorted prints
8¹/₄ yds for backing
1 yd for binding
120" x 120" batting

CUTTING OUT THE PIECES

All measurements include a ¹/₄" seam allowance. Follow
Rotary Cutting, page 144, to cut fabric.

1. **From white solid:** ☐
   - Cut 29 strips 2¹/₄"w. From these strips, cut 516 **squares** 2¹/₄" x 2¹/₄".
   - Cut 19 strips 3³/₄"w. From these strips, cut 202 squares 3³/₄" x 3³/₄". Cut squares twice diagonally to make 808 **triangles**.
   - Cut 2 lengthwise **side inner borders** 3" x 96¹/₂".
   - Cut 2 lengthwise **top/bottom inner borders** 3" x 83¹/₂".
   - From remaining fabric, cut 20 **large squares** 12¹/₂" x 12¹/₂".

2. **From assorted prints:** ◼
   - Cut 111 strips 1³/₄"w. From these strips, cut 332 **pieces** 1³/₄" x 14".

ASSEMBLING THE QUILT TOP

Follow Piecing and Pressing, page 146, to make quilt top.

1. To cut the diamonds for each star, select 2 different print **pieces**. Place **pieces** right sides together, carefully matching raw edges. Referring to **Fig. 1**, align the 45° marking (shown in pink) on the rotary cutting ruler along the lower edge of **pieces**. Cut along right edge of ruler to cut 1 end of the **pieces** at a 45° angle.

Fig. 1

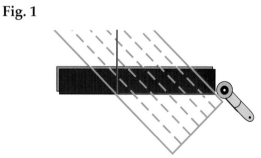

2. Turn cut **pieces** 180° on mat and align the 45° marking on the rotary cutting ruler with the lower edge of the **pieces**. Align the previously cut 45° edge with the 1³/₄" marking on the ruler. Cut at 1³/₄" intervals as shown in **Fig. 2** to cut 4 pairs of **diamonds**.

Fig. 2

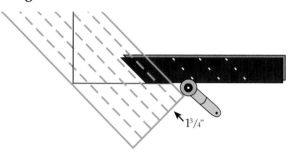

3. Repeat Steps 1 and 2 to cut 166 sets of 4 pairs of **diamonds**. Set aside 38 sets for use in Step 10.

4. Follow **Working with Diamond Shapes**, page 148, to sew 1 set of 4 pairs of **diamonds**, 4 **squares**, and 4 **triangles** together to make **Star Block**. Repeat to make 128 **Star Blocks**.

Star Block (make 128)

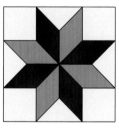

5. Sew 13 **Star Blocks** together to make **Row A**. Make 6 **Row A's**.

Row A (make 6)

6. Sew 2 **Star Blocks** together to make **Unit 1**. Make 25 **Unit 1's**.

Unit 1 (make 25)

7. Sew 5 **Unit 1's** and 4 **large squares** together to make **Row B**. Make 5 **Row B's**.

Row B (make 5)

8. Referring to **Quilt Top Diagram**, page 122, sew **Row A's** and **Row B's** together to make center section of quilt top.
9. Sew **side**, then **top** and **bottom inner borders** to center section.
10. (*Note:* For Steps 10 - 12, follow **Working with Diamond Shapes**, page 148.) Selecting diamonds randomly from those set aside in Step 3, sew 2 **diamonds** and 1 **triangle** together to make **Border Unit**. Make 150 **Border Units** (you will have 4 diamonds left over).

Border Unit (make 150)

11. Sew 34 **Border Units** and 33 **triangles** together to make **Top/Bottom Pieced Border**. Make 2 **Top/Bottom Pieced Borders**.

Top/Bottom Pieced Border (make 2)

12. Sew 41 **Border Units** and 40 **triangles** together to make **Side Pieced Border**. Make 2 **Side Pieced Borders**.

Side Pieced Border (make 2)

13. Sew **Pieced Borders** to top, bottom, and sides of center section of quilt top, beginning and ending seams exactly 1/4" from each corner of quilt top and backstitching at beginning and end of stitching.

14. Fold 1 corner of quilt top diagonally with right sides together, matching outer edges of borders as shown in **Fig. 3**. Beginning at point where previous seams ended, stitch diamonds together, ending seam 1/4" from edge and backstitching.

Fig. 3

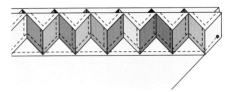

15. Follow Steps 2 - 4 of **Working with Diamond Shapes**, page 148, to add **square** to corner where borders are joined.
16. Repeat Steps 14 and 15 with each remaining corner to complete **Quilt Top**.

COMPLETING THE QUILT

1. Follow **Quilting**, page 151, to mark, layer, and quilt using **Quilting Diagram** as a suggestion. Our quilt is hand quilted.
2. Cut a 34" square of binding fabric. Follow **Binding**, page 155, to bind quilt using 2¹/₂"w bias binding with mitered corners.

Quilting Diagram

121

CURTAIN TIEBACKS

TIEBACK SIZE: 3½" x 25½"

Instructions are for making 2 tiebacks.

SUPPLIES
scraps of 20 assorted print fabrics
⅜ yd of 45"w white solid fabric
3½ yds of 2"w bias strip for welting
3½ yds of ⁷⁄₃₂" cord for welting
¼ yd of 45"w fusible fleece
4 small cabone (drapery) rings

MAKING THE TIEBACKS
*Follow **Rotary Cutting**, page 144, and **Piecing and Pressing**, page 146, to make tiebacks.*

1. From each print, cut 2 rectangles 1¾" x 5" to make a total of 40 rectangles. Place each pair of matching rectangles right sides together, carefully matching raw edges. Follow Steps 1 and 2 of **Assembling the Quilt Top**, page 120, to cut 1 pair of **diamonds** from each pair of rectangles. Separate pairs to make 2 sets of 20 different diamonds.

2. From white solid, cut 10 squares 3¾" x 3¾". Cut squares twice diagonally to make 40 **triangles** (you will need 38 and have 2 left over). Cut 2 squares 2⅛" x 2⅛". Cut squares once diagonally to make 4 **small triangles**.

3. (*Note:* For Steps 3 and 4, follow **Working with Diamond Shapes**, page 148.) Using 1 set of diamonds, sew 2 **diamonds** and 1 **triangle** together to make **Unit 1**; make 10 **Unit 1's**.

Unit 1 (make 10)

4. Sew 10 **Unit 1's**, 9 **triangles**, and 2 **small triangles** together to make 1 **tieback top**.

5. Using second set of diamonds, repeat Steps 3 and 4, arranging diamonds in mirror image, to make second tieback top.

Tieback Tops

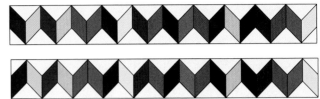

6. Follow Step 2 of **Adding Welting to Pillow Top**, page 158, to make welting. Cut welting into 2 equal lengths.

7. Follow Steps 3 and 4 of **Adding Welting to Pillow Top** to baste welting to each tieback top.

8. Cut 2 **backs** same size as tieback tops. Matching right sides and raw edges, pin and stitch each **tieback top** and **back** together along all edges, stitching as close as possible to welting and leaving an opening for turning.

9. Cut fusible fleece ¼" smaller on all sides than each tieback back. Center fleece on wrong side of each tieback back and follow manufacturer's instructions to fuse in place.

10. Turn right side out; press. Blindstitch opening closed to complete each tieback.

11. Sew 1 ring to back at each end of tiebacks.

QUICK TIP

FITTING A PIECED BORDER

Pieced borders can add wonderful visual interest to your quilt, but with so many pieces and seams, fitting them to your quilt top can be a challenge. Measuring, measuring, and more measuring at critical points will ensure that the quilt top fits together from the center to the very edges.

- *Making pieced borders fit begins when cutting and assembling the center section of the quilt top. Be as accurate as possible in your cutting and pay strict attention to consistently making ¼" seams. Finish each step with careful pressing.*

- *Measure often as you complete the units of the center section of your quilt top to make sure that you are staying on track. By doing so, you can make adjustments as you go. Measure the size of finished blocks, the length of rows, and the size of other units or sections, so that you will finish with the correct size center section.*

- *As you add to the center section, measure to make sure that opposite edges (both sides or top and bottom) remain equal in length. A perfectly symmetrical center section will need fewer adjustments in the lengths of the borders.*

- *After completing ¼ or ½ of your pieced border, measure to see how you are doing. Then, if necessary, you can make small adjustments in the remaining seam allowances.*

CHARMING DISHES COLLECTION

A *delightful geometric design that was popular across America in the early 1800's, the Broken Dishes pattern has always been a favorite way to use up a variety of scrap fabrics. Created with four triangle-squares, each Broken Dishes block is simple enough for even a beginner to create. Because many different fabrics are used for this quilt, our instructions show you how to use a special ruler to quickly rotary cut accurate triangles with ease. Arranging the many-colored blocks together without any sashing creates a lively mosaic that plays upon the light and dark values of the pieces. To visually unite the project, we finished it with a simple outer border that matches a shade used throughout the quilt.*

In the 1860's, quilters began trading scraps of fabric with friends and relatives, using their collections to make "charm quilts" — scrap quilts in which no two pieces were cut from the same fabric. The practice became a fad with Victorians, who adored such sentimental traditions. Legend held that when a maiden had collected exactly 999 scraps for her charm quilt, the young man of her dreams would appear wearing the fabric for her one thousandth piece. On a smaller scale, our charm table topper (below) contains 288 different fabrics. Its blocks are made with triangle-squares that are rotary cut with a special ruler for accuracy. For our wall hanging (opposite), we used luscious hand-dyed fabrics to create subtle shading in our iris appliqués. The motifs are easy to assemble using fusible web and clear nylon thread.

BROKEN DISHES QUILT

SKILL LEVEL: 1 2 3 4 5
BLOCK SIZE: 6½" x 6½"
QUILT SIZE: 72" x 85"

YARDAGE REQUIREMENTS

Yardage is based on 45"w fabric.

 2¾ yds of dark red print

4 - 5 yds of assorted dark print scraps

4 - 5 yds of assorted light print scraps
5¼ yds for backing
1 yd for binding
81" x 96" batting

You will also need:
Easy Angle™ Rotary Cutting Ruler (made by EZ International)

CUTTING OUT THE BORDERS

All measurements include a ¼" seam allowance. Follow Rotary Cutting, page 144, to cut fabric.

1. **From dark red print:**
   - Cut 2 lengthwise strips 3¼" x 69" for **top/bottom borders**.
   - Cut 2 lengthwise strips 3¼" x 88" for **side borders**.

CUTTING OUT THE TRIANGLES

1. To cut triangles, refer to **Fig. 1** to line up left edge of Easy Angle ruler with straight grain of 1 fabric scrap. Cut along bottom and left edges of ruler.

Fig. 1

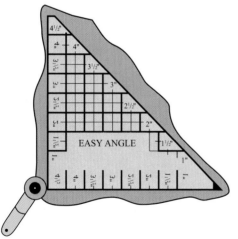

2. Referring to **Fig. 2**, line up bottom edge of ruler with bottom cut edge of fabric; slide ruler to left until 3¾" line (shown in pink) is aligned with left cut edge of fabric. Cut along angled edge of ruler to complete **triangle**.

Fig. 2

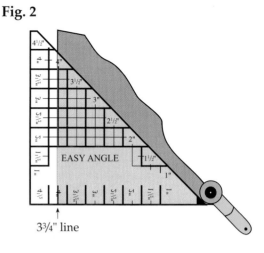

↑
3¾" line

3. Repeat Steps 1 and 2 with remaining scraps to make a total of 480 **dark triangles** and 480 **light triangles**.

dark triangle (cut 480)   **light triangle** (cut 480)

ASSEMBLING THE QUILT TOP

Follow Piecing and Pressing, page 146, to make quilt top.

1. Sew 1 **dark** and 1 **light triangle** together to make **triangle-square**. Make 480 **triangle-squares**.

triangle-square (make 480)

2. Sew 4 **triangle-squares** together to make **Block**. Make 120 **Blocks**.

Block (make 120)

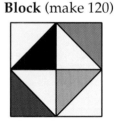

3. Sew 10 **Blocks** together to make **Row**. Make 12 **Rows**.

Row (make 12)

4. Referring to **Quilt Top Diagram**, sew **Rows** together to make center section of quilt top.
5. Follow **Adding Squared Borders**, page 150, to sew **top**, **bottom**, then **side borders** to center section to complete **Quilt Top**.

COMPLETING THE QUILT
1. Follow **Quilting**, page 151, to mark, layer, and quilt. Our quilt is hand quilted in diagonal lines.
2. Cut a 30" square of binding fabric. Follow **Binding**, page 155, to bind quilt using 2¹/₂"w bias binding with mitered corners.

Quilt Top Diagram

CHARM TABLE TOPPER

BLOCK SIZE: 6¹/₂" x 6¹/₂"
TABLE TOPPER SIZE: 45" x 45"

YARDAGE REQUIREMENTS
Yardage is based on 45"w fabric.

- ¹/₂ yd of blue stripe
- ¹/₈ yd of purple dot
- scraps of 144 different light fabrics
- scraps of 144 different dark fabrics
  1³/₈ yds for backing
  ³/₄ yd for binding
  49" x 49" batting

CUTTING OUT THE PIECES
All measurements include a ¹/₄" seam allowance. Follow Rotary Cutting, page 144, to cut fabric.

1. **From blue stripe:**
   - Cut 4 **borders** 3" x 39¹/₂".
2. **From purple dot:**
   - Cut 4 **border corner squares** 3" x 3".
3. **From scraps of light and dark fabrics:**
   - Follow **Cutting Out the Triangles**, page 128, to cut 144 **light triangles** and 144 **dark triangles**.

MAKING THE TABLE TOPPER
Follow Piecing and Pressing, page 146, to make table topper.

1. Sew 1 **light triangle** and 1 **dark triangle** together to make **triangle-square**. Make 144 **triangle-squares**.

triangle-square (make 144)

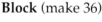

2. Sew 4 **triangle-squares** together to make **Block**. Make 36 **Blocks**.

Block (make 36)

3. Sew 6 **Blocks** together to make **Row**. Make 6 **Rows**.

Row (make 6)

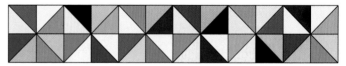

4. Referring to **Table Topper Diagram**, page 130, sew **Rows** together to make center section of table topper.
5. Sew 1 **border** each to top and bottom edges of center section. Sew **border corner squares** to ends of remaining **borders**; sew borders to side edges of center section to complete **Table Topper Top**.
6. Follow **Quilting**, page 151, to mark, layer, and quilt. Our table topper is hand quilted in diagonal lines.
7. Cut a 22" square of binding fabric. Follow **Binding**, page 155, to bind table topper using 2¹/₂"w bias binding with mitered corners.

Table Topper Diagram

IRIS WALL HANGING

SKILL LEVEL: 1 2 3 4 5
BLOCK SIZE: 6½" x 6½"
WALL HANGING SIZE: 26" x 26"

YARDAGE REQUIREMENTS
Yardage is based on 45"w fabric.

⫴ ³/₈ yd of blue stripe

☐ ¼ yd of white print

▓ ⅛ yd of purple dot

◢ scraps of 4 blue solids, 2 green solids, and 1 yellow print for appliqués

◣ 5" x 13" piece *each* of 4 dark blue prints

◺ 5" x 13" piece *each* of 4 light blue prints
⁷/₈ yd for backing
³/₈ yd for binding
30" x 30" batting

You will also need:
transparent monofilament thread for appliqué
paper-backed fusible web

CUTTING OUT THE PIECES
All measurements include a ¼" seam allowance. Follow Rotary Cutting, page 144, to cut fabric unless otherwise indicated.

1. **From blue stripe:** ⫴
   - Cut 4 strips 2"w. From these strips, cut 24 **sashing strips** 2" x 7".

2. **From white print:** ☐
   - Cut 4 **background squares** 7" x 7".

3. **From purple dot:** ▓
   - Cut 1 strip 2"w. From this strip, cut 16 **sashing squares** 2" x 2".

4. **From scraps for appliqués:** ◣
   - Referring to **Appliquéd Block** diagram, follow **Preparing Fusible Appliqués**, page 149, and use patterns, page 131, to cut 4 *each* of **A - I** (cut 2 **H's** and 2 **I's** in reverse).

5. **From *each* dark blue print:** ◣
   - Cut 3 squares 4⅛" x 4⅛". Cut squares once diagonally to make 6 **dark triangles** (you will need 5 and have 1 left over from each print).

6. **From *each* light blue print:** ◺
   - Cut 3 squares 4⅛" x 4⅛". Cut squares once diagonally to make 6 **light triangles** (you will need 5 and have 1 left over from each print).

ASSEMBLING THE WALL HANGING TOP
Follow Piecing and Pressing, page 146, to make wall hanging top.

1. Sew 1 **dark triangle** and 1 **light triangle** together to make **triangle-square**. Make 20 **triangle-squares**.

triangle-squares (make 5 of each)

2. Sew 4 **triangle-squares** together to make **Pieced Block**. Make 5 **Pieced Blocks**.

Pieced Block (make 5)

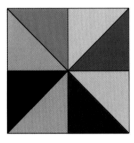

3. Follow **Invisible Appliqué**, page 150, to stitch **appliqués** to **background square** to make **Appliquéd Block**. Make 4 **Appliquéd Blocks**.

Appliquéd Block (make 4)

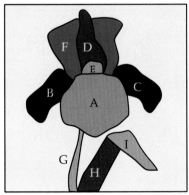

4. Sew 4 **sashing squares** and 3 **sashing strips** together to make **Sashing Row**. Make 4 **Sashing Rows**.

Sashing Row (make 4)

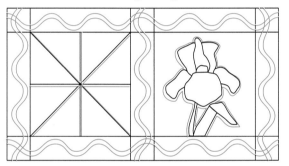

5. Referring to **Wall Hanging Top Diagram**, sew **sashing strips**, **Pieced Blocks**, and **Appliquéd Blocks** together to make 3 **Block Rows**.
6. Sew **Sashing Rows** and **Block Rows** together to complete **Wall Hanging Top**.

COMPLETING THE WALL HANGING
1. Follow **Quilting**, page 151, to mark, layer, and quilt using **Quilting Diagram** as a suggestion. Our wall hanging is hand quilted.
2. Follow **Binding**, page 155, to bind wall hanging using 2¹/₂"w straight-grain binding with overlapped corners.

Wall Hanging Top Diagram

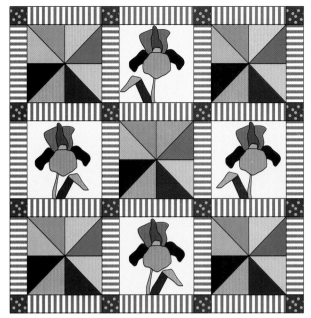

Quilting Diagram

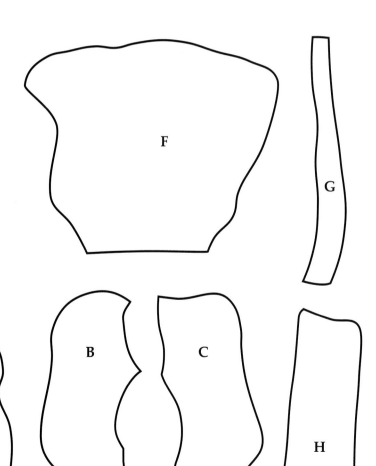

131

LADY OF THE LAKE COLLECTION

The romantic writings of Sir Walter Scott captivated the world in the early nineteenth century. One of his best-known works, Lady of the Lake, was so lyrically enticing that it drew crowds of tourists to the Scottish homeland in which it was set, and it inspired an equally beautiful patchwork design. Our version of the traditional pattern was made using a variety of homey fabrics to create a quaint scrap quilt look. The eclectic arrangement of small "waves" is quite easy to construct — a quick grid technique allows you to make nearly a hundred triangle-squares at a time! For a tranquil touch, the quilt is edged with two simple borders.

A *delightful gift for the lady of the house, our handy apron (opposite) features a variation of the Lady of the Lake block used in the quilt. Strips of a cheerful novelty print accent the bib and the waistband of the gathered skirt. The matching table setting (below) includes a quilt-block place mat, matching napkin, and simple napkin ring.*

LADY OF THE LAKE QUILT

SKILL LEVEL: 1 2 3 4 5
BLOCK SIZE: 6⁷/₈" x 6⁷/₈"
QUILT SIZE: 83" x 102"

Because of the quick methods used to duplicate the scrappy look of the quilt, you will have some pieces left over after assembling the blocks.

YARDAGE REQUIREMENTS
Yardage is based on 45"w fabric.

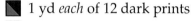 1 yd *each* of 12 dark prints

1 yd *each* of 12 light prints

3¹/₄ yds of green print

3¹/₄ yds of gold print
7⁵/₈ yds for backing
1 yd for binding
90" x 108" batting

CUTTING OUT THE PIECES
All measurements include a ¹/₄" seam allowance. Follow **Rotary Cutting**, *page 144, to cut fabric.*

1. **From *each* dark print:**
   - Cut 2 **large rectangles** 15" x 20" for small triangle-squares.
   - Cut 1 **small rectangle** 12" x 17" for large triangle-squares.
   - From *each* of 8 fabrics, cut 1 square 5" x 5" and 1 square 2¹/₄" x 2¹/₄". Cut squares once diagonally to make 16 **large triangles** and 16 **small triangles**.

2. **From *each* light print:**
   - Cut 2 **large rectangles** 15" x 20" for small triangle-squares.
   - Cut 1 **small rectangle** 12" x 17" for large triangle-squares.
   - From *each* of 8 fabrics, cut 1 square 5" x 5" and 1 square 2¹/₄" x 2¹/₄". Cut squares once diagonally to make 16 **large triangles** and 16 **small triangles**.

3. **From green print:**
   - Cut 2 lengthwise **side inner borders** 2¹/₂" x 105".
   - Cut 2 lengthwise **top/bottom inner borders** 2¹/₂" x 86".

4. **From gold print:**
   - Cut 2 lengthwise **side outer borders** 5¹/₄" x 105".
   - Cut 2 lengthwise **top/bottom outer borders** 5¹/₄" x 86".

ASSEMBLING THE QUILT TOP
Follow **Piecing and Pressing**, *page 146, to make quilt top.*

1. To make small triangle-squares, place 1 light and 1 dark **large rectangle** right sides together. Referring to **Fig. 1**, follow **Making Triangle-Squares**, page 147, to make 96 **small triangle-squares**. Using same color combination, repeat to make a total of 192 **small triangle-squares**.

Fig. 1

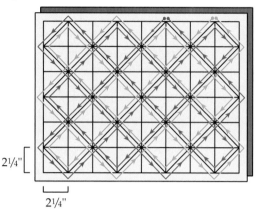

small triangle-square (make 192)

2. Using same color combination as in Step 1, place light and dark **small rectangles** right sides together. Referring to **Fig. 2**, follow **Making Triangle-Squares**, page 147, to make 12 **large triangle-squares**.

Fig. 2

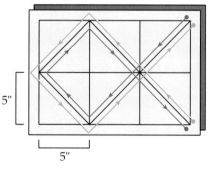

large triangle-square (make 12)

3. Sew 3 **small triangle-squares** together to make **Unit 1**. Make 22 **Unit 1's**. Sew 5 **small triangle-squares** together to make **Unit 2**. Make 22 **Unit 2's**.

Unit 1 (make 22)   **Unit 2** (make 22)

4. Sew 2 **Unit 1's**, 1 **large triangle-square**, and 2 **Unit 2's** together to make **Block**. Make 11 **Blocks**.

Block (make 11)

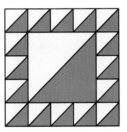

5. Repeat Steps 1 - 4 to make 127 **Blocks**.
6. Sew 1 light print **small triangle** and 3 matching **small triangle-squares** together to make **Unit 3**. Sew 1 light print **small triangle** and 4 matching **small triangle-squares** together to make **Unit 4**.

Unit 3   **Unit 4**

7. Sew **Unit 3**, **Unit 4**, and 1 matching **large triangle** together to make **Partial Block A**.

Partial Block A

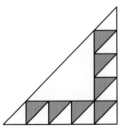

8. Repeat Steps 6 and 7 to make 8 **Partial Block A's**.
9. Using dark print **small triangles** and **large triangles**, repeat Steps 6 and 7 to make 8 **Partial Block B's**.

Partial Block B (make 8)

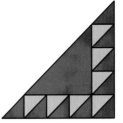

10. Referring to **Assembly Diagram**, page 138, sew **Partial Blocks** and **Blocks** into diagonal rows. Sew rows together to make center section of quilt top.
11. Referring to **Fig. 3**, place ruler on 1 side edge of quilt top with 1/4" marking (shown in pink) lined up with seam intersections; trim sides of **Blocks**.

Fig. 3

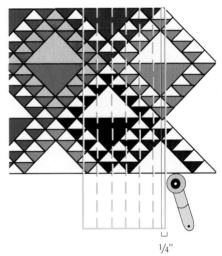

1/4"

12. Sew side **inner** and **outer borders** together along long edges to make 2 **Side Border Units**. Sew **top/bottom inner** and **outer borders** together to make 2 **Top/Bottom Border Units**.
13. Follow **Adding Mitered Borders**, page 151, to sew **Border Units** to center section to complete **Quilt Top**.

COMPLETING THE QUILT

1. Follow **Quilting**, page 151, to mark, layer, and quilt using **Quilting Diagram**, page 139, as a suggestion. Our quilt is hand quilted.
2. Cut a 32" square of binding fabric. Follow **Binding**, page 155, to bind quilt using 2 1/2"w bias binding with mitered corners.

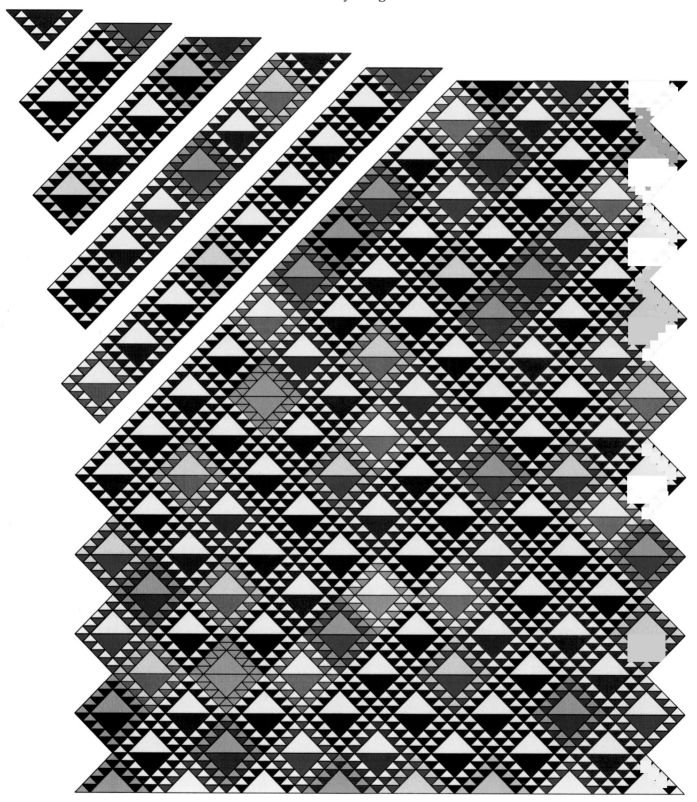

Quilt Top Diagram

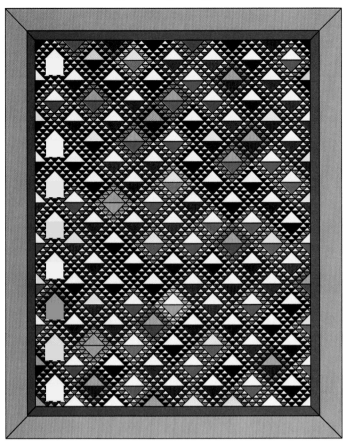

Quilting Diagram

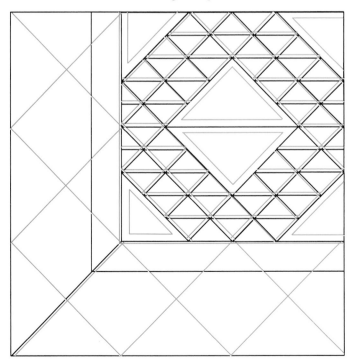

TABLE SETTING

PLACE MAT SIZE: 13" x 20"

Instructions are for making 1 place mat and 1 napkin ring.

YARDAGE REQUIREMENTS

Yardage is based on 45"w fabric.

⬛ ³/₈ yd of black stripe

⬜ ¹/₄ yd of white solid

🟥 ¹/₄ yd of red solid

🏁 ¹/₄ yd of floral print

½ yd for backing

16" x 23" batting

1³/₈" x 5¹/₂" piece of fusible fleece

CUTTING OUT THE PIECES

*All measurements include a ¹/₄" seam allowance. Follow **Rotary Cutting**, page 144, to cut fabric.*

1. **From black stripe:**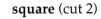
    *   Cut 1 square 11" x 11". Cut square twice diagonally to make 4 **large triangles** (you will need 2 and have 2 left over).
    *   Cut 2 squares 5³/₄" x 5³/₄". Cut squares once diagonally to make 4 **small triangles**. (Squares and triangles must be cut as shown to ensure that stripes run in 1 direction on place mat.)

square (cut 2)

small triangle (cut 4)

2. **From red solid:** 🟥
    *   Cut 1 **rectangle** 8" x 15" for triangle-squares.

3. **From white solid:** ⬜
    *   Cut 1 **rectangle** 8" x 15" for triangle-squares.
    *   Cut 1 **napkin ring backing** 1⁷/₈" x 6".

4. **From floral print:** 🏁
    *   Cut 2 **borders** 2" x 20".
    *   Cut 2 **squares** 4⁵/₈" x 4⁵/₈".

MAKING THE TABLE SETTING

*Follow **Piecing and Pressing**, page 146, to make place mat and napkin ring.*

1. To make small triangle-squares, place red and white **rectangles** right sides together. Referring to **Fig. 1**, follow **Making Triangle-Squares**, page 147, to make 36 **small triangle-squares**.

Fig. 1

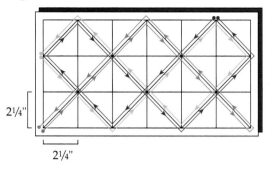

 2¹/₄"

2¹/₄"

small triangle-square (make 36)

NAPKIN RING

1. Sew 4 **small triangle-squares** together to make **Napkin Ring Top**.

Napkin Ring Top (make 1)

2. Center fleece on wrong side of napkin ring top. Follow manufacturer's instructions to fuse in place. Sew napkin ring top and napkin ring backing together along 1 long edge. With right sides together, sew short edges together to make a ring.
3. Press long raw edges of ring ¹/₄" to wrong side; fold napkin ring backing to inside of ring. Blindstitch folded edges together and press.

PLACE MAT

1. Follow Step 3 of **Assembling the Quilt Top**, page 137, to make 4 **Unit 1's** and 4 **Unit 2's**.
2. Follow Step 4 of **Assembling the Quilt Top**, page 137, to make 2 **Blocks**, substituting **squares** for large triangle-squares.
3. Referring to **Assembly Diagram**, sew **Blocks**, **large triangles**, **small triangles**, and **borders** together to make **Place Mat Top**.

4. Cut backing and batting same size as place mat top. Baste batting to wrong side of backing. With right sides together, sew backing and place mat top together, leaving an opening for turning. Cut corners diagonally and turn right side out; blindstitch opening closed and press.
5. Follow **Quilting**, page 151, to quilt in the ditch around outside edge of blocks and along inside edge of borders. Our place mat is machine quilted.

Assembly Diagram

APRON

YARDAGE REQUIREMENTS

Yardage is based on 45"w fabric.

- ⁷/₈ yd of black and white stripe
- ⁵/₈ yd of floral print
- ¹/₄ yd of white solid
- ¹/₄ yd of red solid
  11¹/₄" x 12¹/₄" batting
  11¹/₄" x 12¹/₄" backing

CUTTING OUT THE PIECES

*All measurements include a ¹/₄" seam allowance. Follow **Rotary Cutting**, page 144, to cut fabric.*

1. **From black and white stripe:** ▬
   - Cut 1 **skirt** 25¹/₂" x 35" with stripes running parallel to short edges.
   - Cut 2 squares 5³/₄" x 5³/₄". Cut squares once diagonally to make 4 **triangles**. (Squares and triangles must be cut as shown to ensure that stripes run in 1 direction on apron.)

square (cut 2)

triangle (cut 4)

2. **From floral print:**
   - Cut 2 **ties** 4" x 28".
   - Cut 2 **side borders** 1½" x 10¼".
   - Cut 1 **top border** 1½" x 12¼".
   - Cut 1 **square** 4⅝" x 4⅝".
   - Cut 1 **waistband** 3" x 70", pieced as necessary.

3. **From white solid:** ☐
   - Cut 1 **rectangle** 6" x 10" for triangle-squares.

4. **From red solid:** ■
   - Cut 1 **rectangle** 6" x 10" for triangle-squares.

MAKING THE APRON

*Follow **Piecing and Pressing**, page 146, to make apron.*

1. To make small triangle-squares, place red and white **rectangles** right sides together. Referring to **Fig. 1**, follow **Making Triangle-Squares**, page 147, to make 16 **small triangle-squares**.

Fig. 1

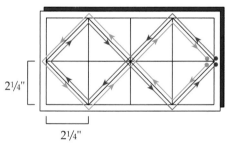

2¼"
2¼"

small triangle-square (make 16)

2. Follow Step 3 of **Assembling the Quilt Top**, page 137, to make 2 **Unit 1's** and 2 **Unit 2's**.

3. Follow Step 4 of **Assembling the Quilt Top**, page 137, to make 1 **Block**, substituting **square** for large triangle-square.

4. Referring to **Assembly Diagram**, sew **Block**, **triangles**, **side borders**, and **top border** together to make apron bib.

Assembly Diagram

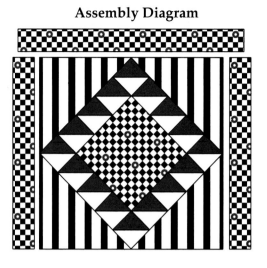

5. Baste batting to wrong side of backing. Place backing and bib right sides together; sew along side and top edges. Turn right side out; press. Baste bottom edges together.

6. Follow **Quilting**, page 151, to quilt in the ditch around outside edge of Block and along inside edges of borders. Our bib is machine quilted.

7. Press each short edge and 1 long edge of **skirt** ½" to wrong side; press ½" to wrong side again and stitch in place. Baste ¼" and ½" from raw edge. Pull basting threads, drawing up gathers to measure 13½".

8. Press each short edge and 1 long edge of **waistband** ½" to wrong side. Matching right sides and raw edges, center gathered edge of skirt on waistband and machine baste ½" from edge. Press seam toward waistband, pressing remaining raw edges of waistband ½" to wrong side. Matching wrong sides and long edges, press waistband in half. Topstitch close to folded edges.

9. Matching centers, lap top of waistband ¼" over basted edge of bib; topstitch in place.

10. For ties, press each short edge of each **tie** ½" to wrong side. Matching wrong sides and long edges, fold each tie in half and press. Fold long raw edges of each tie to center and press. Topstitch close to folded edges of each tie. Blindstitch ties to upper corners on wrong side of bib.

GENERAL INSTRUCTIONS

Complete instructions are given for making each of the quilts and other projects shown in this book. Skill levels indicated for quilts and wall hangings may help you choose the right project. To make your quilting easier and more enjoyable, we encourage you to carefully read all of these general instructions, study the color photographs, and familiarize yourself with the individual project instructions before beginning a project.

QUILTING SUPPLIES

This list includes all the tools you need for basic quick-method quiltmaking, plus additional supplies used for special techniques. Unless otherwise specified, all items may be found in your favorite fabric store or quilt shop.

Batting — Batting is most commonly available in polyester, cotton, or a polyester/cotton blend (see **Choosing and Preparing the Batting**, page 153).

Cutting mat — A cutting mat is a special mat designed to be used with a rotary cutter. A mat that measures approximately 18" x 24" is a good size for most cutting.

Eraser — A soft white fabric eraser or white art eraser may be used to remove pencil marks from fabric. Do not use a colored eraser, as the dye may discolor fabric.

Iron — An iron with both steam and dry settings and a smooth, clean soleplate is necessary for proper pressing.

Marking tools — There are many different types of marking tools available (see **Marking Quilting Lines**, page 152). A silver quilter's pencil is a good marker for both light and dark fabrics.

Masking Tape — Two widths of masking tape, 1"w and 1/4"w, are helpful to have when quilting. The 1"w tape is used to secure the backing fabric to a flat surface when layering the quilt. The 1/4"w tape may be used as a guide when outline quilting.

Needles — Two types of needles are used for hand sewing: *Betweens*, used for quilting, are short and strong for stitching through layered fabric and batting. *Sharps* are longer, thinner needles used for basting and other hand sewing. For *sewing machine needles*, we recommend size 10 to 14 or 70 to 90 universal (sharp-pointed) needles.

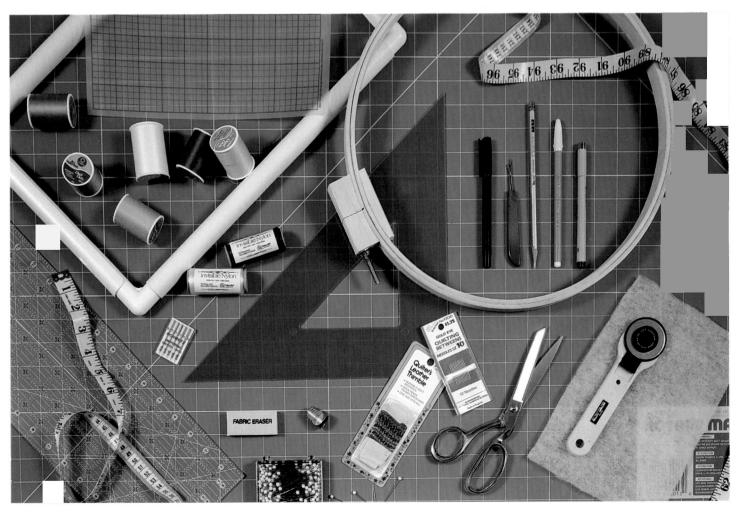

Paper-backed fusible web — This iron-on adhesive with paper backing is used to secure fabric cutouts to another fabric when appliquéing. If the cutouts will be stitched in place, purchase the lighter weight web that will not gum up your sewing machine. A heavier weight web is used for appliqués that are fused in place with no additional stitching.

Permanent fine-point marker — A permanent marker is used to mark templates and stencils and to sign and date quilts. Test marker on fabric to make sure it will not bleed or wash out.

Pins — Straight pins made especially for quilting are extra long with large, round heads. Glass head pins will stand up to occasional contact with a hot iron. Some quilters prefer extra-fine dressmaker's silk pins. If you are machine quilting, you will need a large supply of 1" long (size 01) rust-proof safety pins for pin-basting.

Quilting hoop or frame — Quilting hoops and frames are designed to securely hold the 3 layers of a quilt together while you quilt. Many different types and sizes are available, including round and oval wooden hoops, frames made of rigid plastic pipe, and large floor frames made of either material. A 14" or 16" hoop allows you to quilt in your lap and makes your quilting portable.

Rotary cutter — The rotary cutter is the essential tool for quick-method quilting techniques. The cutter consists of a round, sharp blade mounted on a handle with a retractable blade guard for safety. It should be used only with a cutting mat and rotary cutting ruler. Two sizes are generally available; we recommend the larger (45 mm) size.

Rotary cutting rulers — A rotary cutting ruler is a thick, clear acrylic ruler made specifically for use with a rotary cutter. It should have accurate 1/8" crosswise and lengthwise markings and markings for 45° and 60° angles. A 6" x 24" ruler is a good size for most cutting. An additional 6" x 12" ruler or 12 1/2" square ruler is helpful when cutting wider pieces. Many specialty rulers are available that make specific cutting tasks faster and easier.

Scissors — Although most cutting will be done with a rotary cutter, sharp, high-quality scissors are still needed for some cutting. A separate pair of scissors for cutting paper and plastic is recommended. Smaller scissors are handy for clipping threads.

Seam ripper — A good seam ripper with a fine point is useful for removing stitching.

Sewing machine — A sewing machine that produces a good, even straight stitch is all that is necessary for most quilting. Zigzag stitch capability is necessary for Satin Stitch and Invisible Appliqué. Blindstitch with variable stitch width capability is required for Mock Hand Appliqué. Clean and oil your machine often and keep the tension set properly.

Stabilizer — Commercially made non-woven material or paper stabilizer is placed behind background fabric when doing Satin Stitch or Invisible Appliqué to provide a more stable stitching surface.

Tape measure — A flexible 120" long tape measure is helpful for measuring a quilt top before adding borders.

Template material — Sheets of translucent plastic, often pre-marked with a grid, are made especially for making templates and quilting stencils.

Thimble — A thimble is necessary when hand quilting. Thimbles are available in metal, plastic, or leather and in many sizes and styles. Choose a thimble that fits well and is comfortable.

Thread — Several types of thread are used for quiltmaking: *General-purpose* sewing thread is used for basting, piecing, and some appliquéing. Buy high-quality cotton or cotton-covered polyester thread in light and dark neutrals, such as ecru and grey, for your basic supplies. *Quilting* thread is stronger than general-purpose sewing thread, and some brands have a coating to make them slide more easily through the quilt layers. Some machine appliqué projects in this book use *transparent monofilament* (clear nylon) thread. Use a very fine (.004 mm), soft nylon thread that is not stiff or wiry. Choose clear nylon thread for white or light fabrics or smoke nylon thread for darker fabrics.

Triangle — A large plastic right-angle triangle (available in art and office supply stores) is useful in rotary cutting for making first cuts to "square up" raw edges of fabric and for checking to see that cuts remain at right angles to the fold.

Walking foot — A walking foot or even-feed foot is needed for straight-line machine quilting. This special foot will help all 3 layers of the quilt move at the same rate over the feed dogs to provide a smoother quilted project.

FABRICS

SELECTING FABRICS

For many quilters, choosing fabrics for a new quilt project is one of the most fun, yet challenging, parts of quiltmaking. Photographs of our quilts are excellent guides for choosing the colors for your quilt. You may choose to duplicate the colors in the photograph, or you may use the same light, medium, and dark values in completely different color families. When you change the light and dark value placement in a quilt block, you may come up with a surprising new creation. The most important lesson to learn about fabrics and color is to choose fabrics you love. When you combine several fabrics you are simply crazy about in a quilt, you are sure to be happy with the results!

The yardage requirements listed for each project are based on 45" wide fabric with a "usable" width of 42" after shrinkage and trimming selvages. Your actual usable width will probably vary slightly from fabric to fabric. Though most fabrics will yield 42" or more, if you find a fabric that you suspect will yield a narrower usable width you will need to purchase additional yardage to compensate. Our yardage lengths should be adequate for occasional resquaring of fabric when many cuts are required, but it never hurts to buy a little more fabric for insurance against a narrower usable width, the occasional cutting error, or to have on hand for making coordinating projects.

Choose high-quality, medium-weight, 100% cotton fabrics such as broadcloth or calico. All-cotton fabrics hold a crease better, fray less, and are easier to quilt than cotton/polyester blends. All the fabrics for a quilt should be of comparable weight and weave. Check the end of the fabric bolt for fiber content and width.

PREPARING FABRICS

All fabrics should be washed, dried, and pressed before cutting.

1. To check colorfastness before washing, cut a small piece of the fabric and place in a glass of hot water with a little detergent. Leave fabric in the water for a few minutes. Remove from water and blot fabric with white paper towels. If any color bleeds onto the towels, wash the fabric separately with warm water and detergent, then rinse until the water runs clear. If fabric continues to bleed, choose another fabric.
2. Unfold yardage and separate fabrics by color. To help reduce raveling, use scissors to snip off a small triangle from each corner of your fabric pieces. Machine wash fabrics in warm water with a small amount of mild laundry detergent. Do not use fabric softener. Rinse well and then dry fabrics in the dryer, checking long fabric lengths occasionally to make sure they are not tangling.
3. To make ironing easier, remove fabrics from dryer while they are slightly damp. Refold each fabric lengthwise (as it was on the bolt) with wrong sides together and matching selvages. If necessary, adjust slightly at selvages so that fold lies flat. Press each fabric with a steam iron set on "Cotton."

ROTARY CUTTING

*Based on the idea that you can easily cut strips of fabric and then cut those strips into smaller pieces, rotary cutting has brought speed and accuracy to quiltmaking. Observe safety precautions when using the rotary cutter since it is extremely sharp. Develop a habit of retracting the blade guard **just before** making a cut and closing it **immediately afterward**, before laying down the cutter.*

1. Follow **Preparing Fabrics** to wash, dry, and press fabrics.
2. Cut all strips from the selvage-to-selvage width of the fabric unless otherwise indicated. Place fabric on the cutting mat as shown in **Fig. 1** with the fold of the fabric toward you. To straighten the uneven fabric edge, make the first "squaring up" cut by placing the right edge of the rotary cutting ruler over the left raw edge of the fabric. Place right-angle triangle (or another rotary cutting ruler) with the lower edge carefully aligned with the fold and the left edge against the ruler (**Fig. 1**). Hold the ruler firmly with your left hand, placing your little finger off the left edge of the ruler to anchor it. Remove the triangle, pick up the rotary cutter, and retract the blade guard. Using a smooth, downward motion, make the cut by running the blade of the rotary cutter firmly along the right edge of the ruler (**Fig. 2**). **Always** cut in a direction **away** from your body and **immediately** close the blade guard after each cut.

Fig. 1

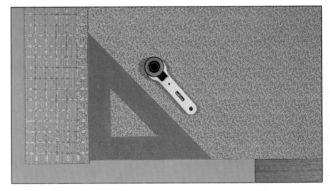

Fig. 2

3. To cut each of the strips required for the project, place the ruler over the cut edge of the fabric, aligning desired marking on the ruler with the cut edge (**Fig. 3**) and then make the cut. When cutting several strips from a single piece of fabric, it is important to occasionally use the ruler and triangle to ensure that cuts are still at a perfect right angle to the fold. If not, repeat Step 2 to straighten.

Fig. 3

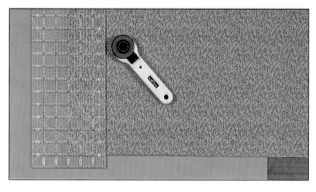

4. To square up selvage ends of a strip before cutting pieces, refer to **Fig. 4** and place folded strip on mat with selvage ends to your right. Aligning a horizontal marking on ruler with 1 long edge of strip, use rotary cutter to trim off selvage to make end of strip square and even (**Fig. 4**). Turn strip (or entire mat) so that cut end is to your left before making subsequent cuts.

Fig. 4

5. Pieces such as rectangles and squares can now be cut from strips. (Cutting other shapes like diamonds is discussed in individual project instructions.) Usually strips remain folded, and pieces are cut in pairs after ends of strips are squared up. To cut squares or rectangles from a strip, place ruler over left end of strip, aligning desired marking on ruler with cut end of strip. To ensure perfectly square cuts, align a horizontal marking on ruler with 1 long edge of strip (**Fig. 5**) before making the cut.

Fig. 5

6. To cut 2 triangles from a square, cut square the size indicated in the project instructions. Cut square once diagonally to make 2 triangles (**Fig. 6**).

Fig. 6

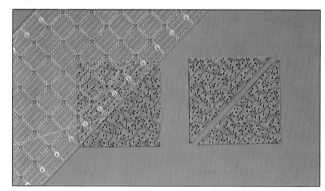

7. To cut 4 triangles from a square, cut square the size indicated in the project instructions. Cut square twice diagonally to make 4 triangles (**Fig. 7**). You may find it helpful to use a small rotary cutting mat so that mat can be turned to make second cut without disturbing fabric pieces.

Fig. 7

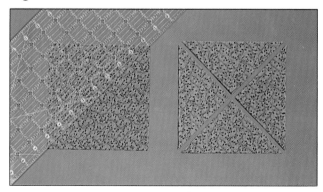

8. After some practice, you may want to try stacking up to 6 fabric layers when making cuts. When stacking strips, match long cut edges and follow Step 4 to square up ends of strip stack. Carefully turn stack (or entire mat) so that squared-up ends are to your left before making subsequent cuts. After cutting, check accuracy of pieces. Some shapes, such as diamonds, are more difficult to cut accurately in stacks.

9. In some cases, strips will be sewn together into strip sets before being cut into smaller units. When cutting a strip set, align a seam in strip set with a horizontal marking on the ruler to maintain square cuts (**Fig. 8**). We do not recommend stacking strip sets for rotary cutting.

Fig. 8

10. Most borders for quilts in this book are cut along the more stable lengthwise grain to minimize wavy edges caused by stretching. To remove selvages before cutting lengthwise strips, place fabric on mat with selvages to your left and squared-up end at bottom of mat. Placing ruler over selvage and using squared-up edge instead of fold, follow Step 2 to cut away selvages as you did raw edges (**Fig. 9**). After making a cut the length of the mat, move the next section of fabric to be cut onto the mat. Repeat until you have removed selvages from required length of fabric.

Fig. 9

11. After removing selvages, place ruler over left edge of fabric, aligning desired marking on ruler with cut edge of fabric. Make cuts as in Step 3. After each cut, move next section of fabric onto mat as in Step 8.

PIECING AND PRESSING

Precise cutting, followed by accurate piecing and careful pressing, will ensure that all the pieces of your quilt top fit together well.

PIECING

Set sewing machine stitch length for approximately 11 stitches per inch. Use a new, sharp needle suited for medium-weight woven fabric.

Use a neutral-colored general-purpose sewing thread (not quilting thread) in the needle and in the bobbin. Stitch first on a scrap of fabric to check upper and bobbin thread tension and make any adjustments necessary.

For good results, it is **essential** that you stitch with an **accurate ¼" seam allowance**. On many sewing machines, the measurement from the needle to the outer edge of the presser foot is ¼". If this is the case with your machine, the presser foot is your best guide. If not, measure ¼" from the needle and mark with a piece of masking tape. Special presser feet that are exactly ¼" wide are also available for most sewing machines.

When piecing, **always** place pieces **right sides together** and **match raw edges**; pin if necessary. (If using straight pins, remove the pins just before they reach the sewing machine needle.)

Chain Piecing

Chain piecing whenever possible will make your work go faster and will usually result in more accurate piecing. Stack the pieces you will be sewing beside your machine in the order you will need them and in a position that will allow you to easily pick them up. Pick up each pair of pieces, carefully place them together as they will be sewn, and feed them into the machine one after the other. Stop between each pair only long enough to pick up the next; don't cut thread between pairs (**Fig. 10**). After all pieces are sewn, cut threads, press, and go on to the next step, chain piecing when possible.

Fig. 10

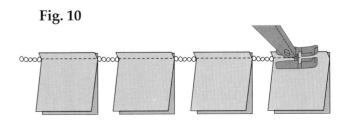

Sewing Strip Sets

When there are several strips to assemble into a strip set, first sew the strips together into pairs, then sew the pairs together to form the strip set. To help avoid distortion, sew 1 seam in 1 direction and then sew the next seam in the opposite direction (**Fig. 11**).

Fig. 11

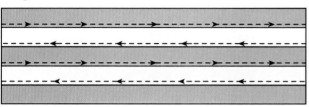

Sewing Across Seam Intersections

When sewing across the intersection of 2 seams, place pieces right sides together and match seams exactly, making sure seam allowances are pressed in opposite directions (**Fig. 12**). To prevent fabric from shifting, you may wish to pin in place.

Fig. 12

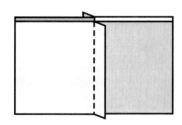

Sewing Sharp Points

To ensure sharp points when joining triangular or diagonal pieces, stitch across the center of the "X" (shown in pink) formed on the wrong side by previous seams (**Fig. 13**).

Fig. 13

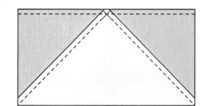

Sewing Bias Seams

Care should be used in handling and stitching bias edges, since they stretch easily. After sewing the seam, carefully press seam allowances to 1 side, making sure not to stretch the fabric.

Making Triangle-Squares

The grid method for making triangle-squares is faster and more accurate than cutting and sewing individual triangles. Stitching before cutting the triangle-squares apart also prevents stretching the bias edges.

1. Follow project instructions to cut rectangles or squares of fabric for making triangle-squares. Place the indicated pieces right sides together and press.
2. On the wrong side of the lighter fabric, draw a grid of squares similar to that shown in **Fig. 14**. The size and number of squares will be given in the project instructions.

Fig. 14

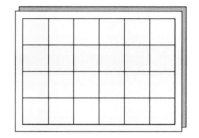

3. Following the example given in the project instructions, draw 1 diagonal line through each square in the grid (**Fig. 15**).

Fig. 15

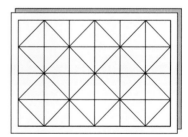

4. Stitch 1/4" on each side of all diagonal lines. For accuracy, it may be helpful to first draw your stitching lines onto the fabric, especially if your presser foot is not your 1/4" guide. In some cases, stitching may be done in a single continuous line. Project instructions include a diagram similar to **Fig. 16** which shows stitching lines and the direction of the stitching.

Fig. 16

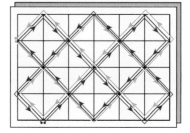

147

5. Use rotary cutter and ruler to cut along all drawn lines of the grid. Each square of the grid will yield 2 triangle-squares (**Fig. 17**).

Fig. 17

6. Carefully press triangle-squares open, pressing seam allowances toward darker fabric. Trim off points of seam allowances that extend beyond edges of triangle-square (see **Fig. 22**).

Working with Diamond Shapes

Piecing diamonds requires special handling. For best results, carefully follow the steps below to assemble the diamond sections of a block.

1. When sewing 2 diamond pieces together, place pieces right sides together, carefully matching edges; pin. Mark a small dot ¹/₄" from corner of 1 piece as shown in **Fig. 18**. Stitch pieces together in the direction shown, stopping at center of dot and backstitching.

Fig. 18

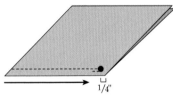

2. For best results, add side triangles, then corner squares to diamond sections. Mark corner of each piece to be set in with a small dot (**Fig. 19**).

Fig. 19

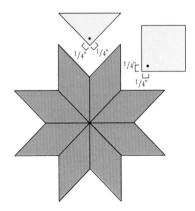

3. To sew first seam, match right sides and pin the triangle or square to the diamond on the left. Stitch seam from the outer edge to the dot, backstitching at the dot; clip threads (**Fig. 20**).

Fig. 20

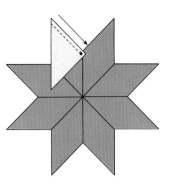

4. To sew the second seam, pivot the added triangle or square to match raw edges of next diamond. Beginning at dot, take 2 or 3 stitches, then backstitch, making sure not to backstitch into previous seam allowance. Continue stitching to outer edge (**Fig. 21**).

Fig. 21

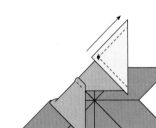

Trimming Seam Allowances

When sewing with diamond or triangle pieces, some seam allowances may extend beyond the edges of the sewn pieces. Trim away "dog ears" that extend beyond the edges of the sewn pieces (**Fig. 22**).

Fig. 22

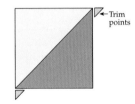

PRESSING

Use a steam iron set on "Cotton" for all pressing. Press as you sew, taking care to prevent small folds along seamlines. Seam allowances are almost always pressed to one side, usually toward the darker fabric. However, to reduce bulk it may occasionally be necessary to press seam allowances toward the lighter fabric or even to press them open. In order to prevent a dark fabric seam allowance from showing through a light fabric, trim the darker seam allowance slightly narrower than the lighter seam allowance. To press long seams, such as those in long strip sets, without curving or other distortion, lay strips across the width of the ironing board.

MACHINE APPLIQUÉ

The projects in this book use either Satin Stitch Appliqué, which is done using a coordinating or contrasting thread, or Invisible Appliqué, which is an adaptation of the satin stitch method. Invisible Appliqué features a tiny zigzag stitch using transparent monofilament thread. Preparation of the appliqué pieces is the same for both types of machine appliqué.

PREPARING FUSIBLE APPLIQUÉS

To make it possible to use our speedy machine appliqué methods, patterns are printed in reverse. White or light-colored fabrics may need to be lined with fusible interfacing before applying fusible web to prevent darker fabrics from showing through.

1. Place paper-backed fusible web, web side down, over appliqué pattern. Use a pencil to trace pattern onto paper side of web as many times as indicated in project instructions for a single fabric. Repeat for additional patterns and fabrics.
2. Follow manufacturer's instructions to fuse traced patterns to wrong side of fabrics. Do not remove paper backing.
3. Some projects may have pieces that are given as measurements (such as a 2" x 4" rectangle) instead of drawn patterns. Fuse web to wrong side of the fabrics indicated for these pieces.
4. Use scissors to cut out appliqué pieces along traced lines; use rotary cutting equipment to cut out appliqué pieces given as measurements. Remove paper backing from all pieces.

SATIN STITCH APPLIQUÉ

A good satin stitch is a smooth, almost solid line of zigzag stitching that covers the raw edges of appliqué pieces. Designs with layered appliqué pieces should be stitched beginning with the bottom pieces and ending with the pieces on top.

1. Referring to diagram and/or photo, arrange appliqués on the background fabric and follow manufacturer's instructions to fuse in place.
2. Pin a stabilizer, such as paper or any of the commercially available products, on wrong side of background fabric before stitching appliqués in place.
3. Thread needle of sewing machine with general purpose thread that coordinates or contrasts with appliqué fabric. Use thread that matches the background fabric in the bobbin for all stitching. Set sewing machine for a medium width (approximately 1/8") zigzag stitch and a very short stitch length. You may find that loosening the top tension slightly will yield a smoother stitch.

4. Beginning on as straight an edge as possible, position fabric so that most of the satin stitch will be on the appliqué piece. Do not backstitch; hold upper thread toward you and sew over it 2 or 3 stitches to anchor thread. Following Steps 5 - 8 for corners and curves, stitch over exposed raw edges of appliqué pieces, changing thread colors as necessary.
5. (*Note:* Dots on **Figs. 23 - 28** indicate where to leave needle in fabric when pivoting.) For **outside corners**, stitch just past the corner, stopping with the needle in **background** fabric (**Fig. 23**). Raise presser foot. Pivot project, lower presser foot, and stitch adjacent side (**Fig. 24**).

Fig. 23   **Fig. 24**

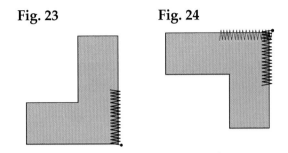

6. For **inside corners**, stitch just past the corner, stopping with the needle in **appliqué** fabric (**Fig. 25**). Raise presser foot. Pivot project, lower presser foot, and stitch adjacent side (**Fig. 26**).

Fig. 25   **Fig. 26**

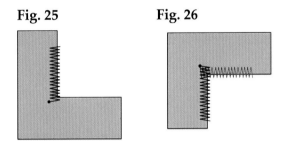

7. When stitching **outside** curves, stop with needle in **background** fabric. Raise presser foot and pivot project as needed. Lower presser foot and continue stitching, pivoting as often as necessary to follow curve (**Fig. 27**).

Fig. 27

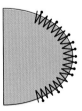

8. When stitching **inside** curves, stop with needle in **appliqué** fabric. Raise presser foot and pivot project as needed. Lower presser foot and continue stitching, pivoting as often as necessary to follow curve (**Fig. 28**).

Fig. 28

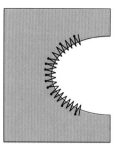

9. Do not backstitch at end of stitching. Pull threads to wrong side of background fabric; knot thread and trim ends.
10. Carefully tear away stabilizer.

INVISIBLE APPLIQUÉ

Transparent monofilament (clear nylon) thread is available in 2 colors: clear and smoke. Use clear on white or very light fabrics and smoke on darker fabrics.

1. Referring to diagram and/or photo, arrange appliqués on the background fabric and follow manufacturer's instructions to fuse in place.
2. Pin a stabilizer, such as paper or any of the commercially available products, on wrong side of background fabric before stitching appliqués in place.
3. Thread sewing machine with transparent monofilament thread. Use general-purpose thread that matches background fabric in bobbin.
4. Set sewing machine for a very narrow (approximately 1/16") zigzag stitch and a short stitch length. You may find that loosening the top tension slightly will yield a smoother stitch.
5. Begin by stitching 2 or 3 stitches in place (drop feed dogs or set stitch length at 0) to anchor thread. Most of the zigzag stitch should be done on the appliqué with the right edge of the stitch falling at the very outside edge of the appliqué piece. Follow Steps 5 - 8 of Satin Stitch Appliqué, page 149, to stitch over all exposed raw edges of appliqué pieces.
6. End stitching by sewing 2 or 3 stitches in place to anchor thread. Trim thread ends close to fabric.
7. Carefully tear away stabilizer.

BORDERS

Borders cut along the lengthwise grain will lie flatter than borders cut along the crosswise grain. In most cases, our instructions for cutting borders for bed-size quilts include an extra 2" of length at each end for "insurance;" borders will be trimmed after measuring completed center section of quilt top.

ADDING SQUARED BORDERS

1. Mark the center of each edge of quilt top.
2. Squared borders are usually added to top and bottom, then side edges of the center section of a quilt top. To add top and bottom borders, measure across center of quilt top to determine length of borders (**Fig. 29**). Trim top and bottom borders to the determined length.

Fig. 29

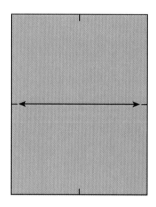

3. Mark center of 1 long edge of top border. Matching center marks and raw edges, pin border to quilt top, easing in any fullness; stitch. Repeat for bottom border.
4. Measure center of quilt top, including attached borders, to determine length of side borders. Trim side borders to the determined length. Repeat Step 3 to add borders to quilt top (**Fig. 30**).

Fig. 30

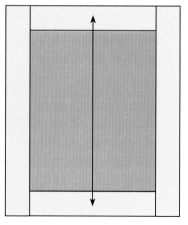

ADDING MITERED BORDERS

1. Mark the center of each edge of quilt top.
2. Mark center of 1 long edge of top border. Measure across center of quilt top (see **Fig. 29**). Matching center marks and raw edges, pin border to center of quilt top edge. From center of border, measure out ½ the width of the quilt top in both directions and mark. Match marks on border with corners of quilt top and pin. Easing in any fullness, pin border to quilt top between center and corners. Sew border to quilt top, beginning and ending seams **exactly** ¼" from each corner of quilt top and backstitching at beginning and end of stitching (**Fig. 31**).

Fig. 31

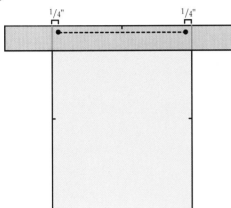

3. Repeat Step 2 to sew bottom, then side borders, to center section of quilt top. To temporarily move first 2 borders out of the way, fold and pin ends as shown in **Fig. 32**.

Fig. 32

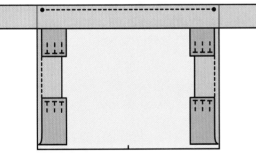

4. Fold 1 corner of quilt top diagonally with right sides together and matching edges. Use ruler to mark stitching line as shown in **Fig. 33**. Pin borders together along drawn line. Sew on drawn line, backstitching at beginning and end of stitching (**Fig. 34**).

Fig. 33

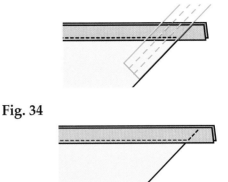

Fig. 34

5. Turn mitered corner right side up. Check to make sure corner will lie flat with no gaps or puckers.
6. Trim seam allowance to ¼"; press to 1 side.
7. Repeat Steps 4 - 6 to miter each remaining corner.

QUILTING

Quilting holds the 3 layers (top, batting, and backing) of the quilt together and may be done by hand or machine. Our project instructions tell you which method is used on our projects and show you quilting diagrams that can be used as suggestions for marking quilting designs. Because marking, layering, and quilting are interrelated and may be done in different orders depending on circumstances, please read this entire section, pages 151 - 154, before beginning the quilting process on your project.

TYPES OF QUILTING

In the Ditch

Quilting very close to a seamline (**Fig. 35**) or appliqué (**Fig. 36**, page 152) is called "in the ditch" quilting. This type of quilting does not need to be marked and is indicated on our quilting diagrams with blue lines close to seamlines. When quilting in the ditch, quilt on the side **opposite** the seam allowance.

Fig. 35

Fig. 36

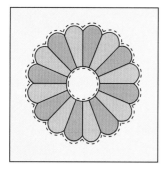

Outline Quilting

Quilting approximately ¹/₄" from a seam or appliqué is called "outline" quilting (**Fig. 37**). This type of quilting is indicated on our quilting diagrams by blue lines a short distance from seamlines. Outline quilting may be marked, or you may place ¹/₄"w masking tape along seamlines and quilt along the opposite edge of the tape. (Do not leave tape on quilt longer than necessary, since it may leave an adhesive residue.)

Fig. 37

Ornamental Quilting

Quilting decorative lines or designs is called "ornamental" quilting (**Fig. 38**). Ornamental quilting is indicated on our quilting diagrams by blue lines. This type of quilting should be marked before you baste quilt layers together.

Fig. 38

MARKING QUILTING LINES

Fabric marking pencils, various types of chalk markers, and fabric marking pens with inks that disappear with exposure to air or water are readily available and work well for different applications. Lead pencils work well on light-colored fabric, but marks may be difficult to remove. White pencils work well on dark-colored fabric, and silver pencils show up well on many colors. Since chalk rubs off easily, it's a good choice if you are marking as you quilt. Fabric marking pens make more durable and visible markings, but the marks should be carefully removed according to manufacturer's instructions. Press down only as hard as necessary to make a visible line.

When you choose to mark your quilt, whether before or after the layers are basted together, is also a factor in deciding which marking tool to use. If you mark with chalk or a chalk pencil, handling the quilt during basting may rub off the markings. Intricate or ornamental designs may not be practical to mark as you quilt; mark these designs before basting using a more durable marker.

To choose marking tools, take all these factors into consideration and **test** different markers **on scrap fabric** until you find the one that gives the desired result.

USING QUILTING STENCILS

A wide variety of pre-cut quilting stencils, as well as entire books of quilting patterns, are available at your local quilt shop or fabric store. Wherever you draw your quilting inspiration from, using a stencil makes it easier to mark intricate or repetitive designs on your quilt top.

1. To make a stencil from a pattern, center template plastic over pattern and use a permanent marker to trace pattern onto plastic.
2. Use a craft knife with a single or double blade to cut narrow slits along traced lines (**Fig. 39**).

Fig. 39

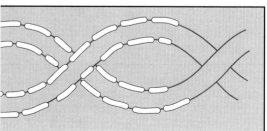

3. Use desired marking tool and stencil to mark quilting lines.

CHOOSING AND PREPARING THE BACKING

To allow for the quilt top shifting slightly during quilting, the backing should be approximately 4" larger on all sides for a bed-size quilt top or approximately 2" larger on all sides for a wall hanging. Yardage requirements listed for quilt backings are calculated for 45"w fabric. If you are making a bed-size quilt, using 90"w or 108"w fabric for the backing may eliminate piecing. To piece a backing using 45"w fabric, use the following instructions.

1. Measure length and width of quilt top; add 8" (4" for a wall hanging) to each measurement.
2. If quilt top is 76"w or less, cut backing fabric into 2 lengths slightly longer than the determined **length** measurement. Trim selvages. Place lengths with right sides facing and sew long edges together, forming a tube (**Fig. 40**). Match seams and press along 1 fold (**Fig. 41**). Cut along pressed fold to form a single piece (**Fig. 42**).

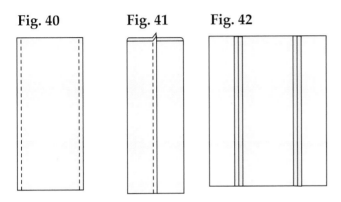

Fig. 40 **Fig. 41** **Fig. 42**

3. If quilt top is more than 76"w, cut backing fabric into 3 lengths slightly longer than the determined **width** measurement. Trim selvages. Sew long edges together to form a single piece.
4. Trim backing to correct size, if necessary, and press seam allowances open.

CHOOSING AND PREPARING THE BATTING

Choosing the right batting will make your quilting job easier. For fine hand quilting, choose a low-loft batting in any of the fiber types described below. Machine quilters will want to choose a low-loft batting that is all cotton or a cotton/polyester blend because the cotton helps "grip" the layers of the quilt. If the quilt is to be tied, a high-loft batting, sometimes called extra-loft or fat batting, is a good choice.

Batting is available in many different fibers. Bonded polyester batting is one of the most popular batting types. It is treated with a protective coating to stabilize the fibers and to reduce "bearding," a process where batting fibers work their way out through the quilt fabrics. Other batting options include cotton/polyester batting, which combines the best of both polyester and cotton battings; all cotton batting, which must be quilted more closely than polyester batting; and wool and silk battings, which are generally more expensive and are usually only dry-cleanable.

Whichever batting you choose, read the manufacturer's instructions closely for any special notes on care or preparation. When you're ready to use your chosen batting in a project, cut the batting the same size as the prepared backing.

LAYERING THE QUILT

1. Examine wrong side of quilt top closely and trim any seam allowances and clip any threads that may show through the front of the quilt. Press quilt top.
2. If quilt top is to be marked before layering, mark quilting lines (see **Marking Quilting Lines**, page 152).
3. Place backing **wrong** side up on a flat surface. Use masking tape to tape edges of backing to surface. Place batting on wrong side of backing fabric. Smooth batting gently, being careful not to stretch or tear. Center quilt top **right** side up on batting.
4. If hand quilting, begin in the center and work toward the outer edges to hand baste all layers together. Use long stitches and place basting lines approximately 4" apart (**Fig. 43**). Smooth fullness or wrinkles toward outer edges.

Fig. 43

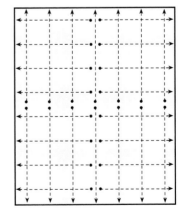

5. If machine quilting, use 1" rust-proof safety pins to "pin-baste" all layers together, spacing pins approximately 4" apart. Begin at the center and work toward the outer edges to secure all layers. If possible, place pins away from areas that will be quilted, although pins may be removed as needed when quilting.

HAND QUILTING

The quilting stitch is a basic running stitch that forms a broken line on the quilt top and backing. Stitches on the quilt top and backing should be straight and equal in length.

1. Secure center of quilt in hoop or frame. Check quilt top and backing to make sure they are smooth. To help prevent puckers, always begin quilting in the center of the quilt and work toward the outside edges.

2. Thread needle with an 18" - 20" length of quilting thread; knot 1 end. Using a thimble, insert needle into quilt top and batting approximately ¹⁄₂" from where you wish to begin quilting. Bring needle up at the point where you wish to begin (**Fig. 44**); when knot catches on quilt top, give thread a quick, short pull to "pop" knot through fabric into batting (**Fig. 45**).

Fig. 44

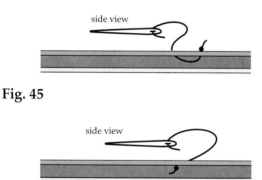

Fig. 45

3. Holding the needle with your sewing hand and placing your other hand underneath the quilt, use thimble to push the tip of the needle down through all layers. As soon as needle touches your finger underneath, use that finger to push only the tip of the needle back up through the layers to top of quilt. (The amount of the needle showing above the fabric determines the length of the quilting stitch.) Referring to **Fig. 46**, rock the needle up and down, taking 3 - 6 stitches before bringing the needle and thread completely through the layers. Check the back of the quilt to make sure stitches are going through all layers. When quilting through a seam allowance or quilting a curve or corner, you may need to take 1 stitch at a time.

Fig. 46

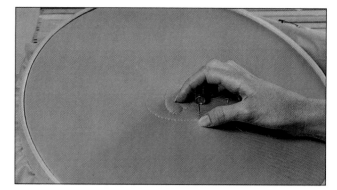

4. When you reach the end of your thread, knot thread close to the fabric and "pop" knot into batting; clip thread close to fabric.

5. Stop and move your hoop as often as necessary. You do not have to tie a knot every time you move your hoop; you may leave the thread dangling and pick it up again when you return to that part of the quilt.

MACHINE QUILTING

The machine-quilted projects in this book feature straight-line quilting, which requires a walking foot or even-feed foot. The term "straight-line" is somewhat deceptive, since curves (especially gentle ones) as well as straight lines can be stitched with this technique.

1. Wind your sewing machine bobbin with general-purpose thread that matches the quilt backing. Do not use quilting thread. Thread the needle of your machine with transparent monofilament thread if you want your quilting to blend with your quilt top fabrics. Use decorative thread, such as a metallic or contrasting colored general-purpose thread, when you want the quilting lines to stand out more. Set the stitch length for 6 - 10 stitches per inch and attach the walking foot to sewing machine.

2. After pin-basting, decide which section of the quilt will have the longest continuous quilting line, oftentimes the area from center top to center bottom. Leaving the area where you will place your first line of quilting exposed, roll up each edge of the quilt to help reduce the bulk, keeping fabrics smooth. Smaller projects may not need to be rolled.

3. Start stitching at beginning of longest quilting line, using very short stitches for the first ¹⁄₄" to "lock" beginning of quilting line. Stitch across project, using one hand on each side of the walking foot to slightly spread the fabric and to guide the fabric through the machine. Lock stitches at end of quilting line.

4. Continue machine quilting, stitching the longer quilting lines first to stabilize the quilt before moving on to other areas.

BINDING

Binding encloses the raw edges of your quilt. Because of its stretchiness, bias binding works well for binding projects with curves or rounded corners and tends to lie smooth and flat in any given circumstance. It is also more durable than other types of binding. Binding may also be cut from the straight lengthwise or crosswise grain of the fabric. You will find that straight-grain binding works well for projects with straight edges.

MAKING CONTINUOUS BIAS STRIP BINDING

Bias strips for binding can simply be cut and pieced to the desired length. However, when a long length of binding is needed, the "continuous" method is quick and accurate.

1. Cut a square from binding fabric the size indicated in the project instructions. Cut square in half diagonally to make 2 triangles.
2. With right sides together and using a 1/4" seam allowance, sew triangles together (**Fig. 47**); press seam allowance open.

Fig. 47

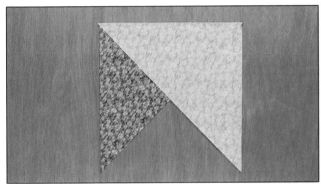

3. On wrong side of fabric, draw lines the width of the binding as specified in the project instructions, usually 21/2" (**Fig. 48**). Cut off any remaining fabric less than this width.

Fig. 48

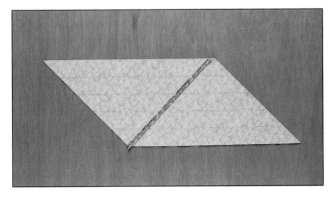

4. With right sides inside, bring short edges together to form a tube; match raw edges so that first drawn line of top section meets second drawn line of bottom section (**Fig. 49**).

Fig. 49

5. Carefully pin edges together by inserting pins through drawn lines at the point where drawn lines intersect, making sure the pins go through intersections on both sides. Using a 1/4" seam allowance, sew edges together. Press seam allowance open.
6. To cut continuous strip, begin cutting along first drawn line (**Fig. 50**). Continue cutting along drawn line around tube.

Fig. 50

7. Trim ends of bias strip square.
8. Matching wrong sides and raw edges, press bias strip in half lengthwise to complete binding.

MAKING STRAIGHT-GRAIN BINDING

1. To determine length of strip needed if attaching binding with mitered corners, measure edges of the quilt and add 12".
2. To determine lengths of strips needed if attaching binding with overlapped corners, measure each edge of quilt; add 3" to each measurement.
3. Cut lengthwise or crosswise strips of binding fabric the determined length and the width called for in the project instructions. Strips may be pieced to achieve the necessary length.
4. Matching wrong sides and raw edges, press strip(s) in half lengthwise to complete binding.

ATTACHING BINDING WITH MITERED CORNERS

1. Press 1 end of binding diagonally (**Fig. 51**).

Fig. 51

2. Lay binding around quilt to make sure that seams in binding will not end up at a corner. Adjust placement if necessary. Matching raw edges of binding to raw edge of quilt top and beginning with pressed end several inches from a corner, pin binding to right side of quilt along 1 edge.
3. When you reach the first corner, mark ¹/₄" from corner of quilt top (**Fig. 52**).

Fig. 52

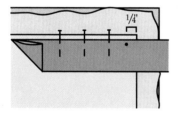

4. Using a ¹/₄" seam allowance, sew binding to quilt, backstitching at beginning of stitching and when you reach the mark (**Fig. 53**). Lift needle out of fabric and clip thread.

Fig. 53

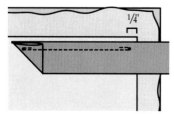

5. Fold binding as shown in **Figs. 54** and **55** and pin binding to adjacent side, matching raw edges. When you reach the next corner, mark ¹/₄" from edge of quilt top.

Fig. 54   **Fig. 55**

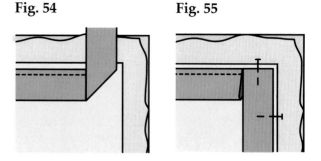

6. Backstitching at edge of quilt top, sew pinned binding to quilt (**Fig. 56**); backstitch when you reach the next mark. Lift needle out of fabric and clip thread.

Fig. 56

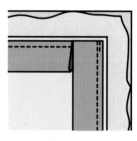

7. Repeat Steps 5 and 6 to continue sewing binding to quilt until binding overlaps beginning end by approximately 2". Trim excess binding.
8. If using 2¹/₂"w binding (finished size ¹/₂"), trim backing and batting a scant ¹/₄" larger than quilt top so that batting and backing will fill the binding when it is folded over to the quilt backing. If using narrower binding, trim backing and batting even with edges of quilt top.
9. On 1 edge of quilt, fold binding over to quilt backing and pin pressed edge in place, covering stitching line (**Fig. 57**). On adjacent side, fold binding over, forming a mitered corner (**Fig. 58**). Repeat to pin remainder of binding in place.

Fig. 57   **Fig. 58**

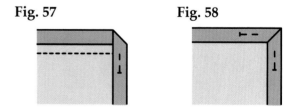

10. Blindstitch binding to backing, taking care not to stitch through to front of quilt.

ATTACHING BINDING WITH OVERLAPPED CORNERS

1. Matching raw edges and using a ¼" seam allowance, sew a length of binding to top and bottom edges on right side of quilt.
2. If using 2½"w binding (finished size ½"), trim backing and batting from top and bottom edges a scant ¼" larger than quilt top so that batting and backing will fill the binding when it is folded over to the quilt backing. If using narrower binding, trim backing and batting even with edges of quilt top.
3. Trim ends of binding even with edges of quilt top. Fold binding over to quilt backing and pin pressed edges in place, covering stitching line (**Fig. 59**); blindstitch binding to backing.

Fig. 59

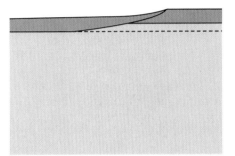

4. Leaving approximately 1½" of binding at each end, stitch a length of binding to each side edge of quilt. Trim backing and batting as in Step 2.
5. Trim each end of binding ½" longer than bound edge. Fold each end of binding over to quilt backing (**Fig. 60**); pin in place. Fold binding over to quilt backing and blindstitch in place, taking care not to stitch through to front of quilt.

Fig. 60

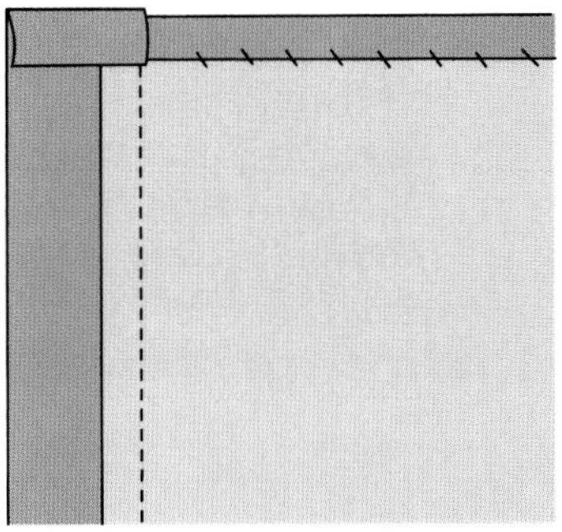

MAKING A HANGING SLEEVE

Attaching a hanging sleeve to the back of your wall hanging or quilt before the binding is added allows you to display your completed project on a wall.

1. Measure the width of the wall hanging top and subtract 1". Cut a piece of fabric 7"w by the determined measurement.
2. Press short edges of fabric piece ¼" to wrong side; press edges ¼" to wrong side again and machine stitch in place.
3. Matching wrong sides, fold piece in half lengthwise to form a tube.
4. Follow project instructions to sew binding to quilt top and to trim backing and batting. Before blindstitching binding to backing, match raw edges and stitch hanging sleeve to center top edge on back of wall hanging.
5. Finish binding wall hanging, treating the hanging sleeve as part of the backing.
6. Blindstitch bottom of hanging sleeve to backing, taking care not to stitch through to front of quilt.
7. Insert dowel or slat into hanging sleeve.

SIGNING AND DATING YOUR QUILT

Your completed quilt is a work of art and should be treated as such. And like any artist, you should sign and date your work. There are many different ways to do this, and you should pick a method of signing and dating that reflects the quilt, the occasion for which it was made, and your own particular talents.

The following suggestions may give you an idea for recording the history of your quilt for future generations.

- Embroider your name, the date, and any additional information on the quilt top or backing. You may choose floss colors that closely match the fabric you are working on, such as white floss on a white border, or contrasting colors may be used.
- Make a label from muslin and use a permanent marker to write your information. Your label may be as plain or as fancy as you wish. Then stitch the label to the back of the quilt.
- Chart a cross-stitch label design that includes the information you wish and stitch it in colors that complement the quilt. Stitch the finished label to the quilt backing.

PILLOW FINISHING

Any quilt block may be made into a pillow. If desired, you may add welting and/or a ruffle to the pillow top before sewing the pillow top and back together.

ADDING WELTING TO PILLOW TOP

1. To make welting, use bias strip indicated in project instructions. (Or, measure edges of pillow top and add 4". Measure diameter of cord and add 1". Cut a bias strip of fabric the determined measurement, piecing if necessary.)
2. Lay cord along center of bias strip on wrong side of fabric; fold strip over cord. Using a zipper foot, machine baste along length of strip close to cord. Trim seam allowance to the width you will use to sew pillow top and back together (see Step 2 of **Making the Pillow**).
3. Matching raw edges and beginning and ending 3" from ends of welting, baste welting to right side of pillow top. To make turning corners easier, clip seam allowance of welting at pillow top corners.
4. Remove approximately 3" of seam at 1 end of welting; fold fabric away from cord. Trim remaining end of welting so that cord ends meet exactly. Fold short edge of welting fabric 1/2" to wrong side; fold fabric back over area where ends meet (**Fig. 61**). Baste remainder of welting to pillow top close to cord.

Fig. 61

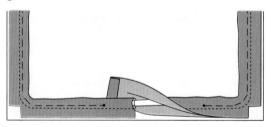

5. Follow **Making the Pillow** to complete pillow.

ADDING RUFFLE TO PILLOW TOP

1. To make ruffle, use fabric strip indicated in project instructions. (Or, to determine length of ruffle fabric, measure edges of pillow top and multiply by 2. To determine width of ruffle fabric, multiply desired finished width by 2. Add 1" to width measurement if using a 1/2" seam allowance to complete pillow or 1/2" to measurement if using a 1/4" seam allowance [see Step 2 of **Making the Pillow**]. Cut a strip of fabric the determined measurements, piecing if necessary.)

2. Matching right sides, use a 1/4" seam allowance to sew short edges of ruffle together to form a large circle; press seam allowance open. To fold ruffle in half, match raw edges and fold 1 raw edge of fabric to inside of circle to meet remaining raw edge of fabric; press.
3. To gather ruffle, place quilting thread 1/4" from raw edge of ruffle. Using a medium width zigzag stitch with medium stitch length, stitch over quilting thread, being careful not to catch quilting thread in stitching. Pull quilting thread, drawing up gathers to fit pillow top.
4. Matching raw edges, baste ruffle to right side of pillow top.
5. Follow **Making the Pillow** to complete pillow.

MAKING THE PILLOW

1. For pillow back, cut a piece of fabric the same size as pieced and quilted pillow top.
2. Place pillow back and pillow top right sides together. The seam allowance width you use will depend on the construction of the pillow top. If the pillow top has borders where the finished width of the border is not crucial, use a 1/2" seam allowance for durability. If the pillow top is pieced where a wider seam allowance would interfere with the design, use a 1/4" seam allowance. Using the determined seam allowance (or stitching as close as possible to welting), sew pillow top and back together, leaving an opening at bottom edge for turning.
3. Turn pillow right side out, carefully pushing corners outward. Stuff with polyester fiberfill or pillow form and sew final closure by hand.

GLOSSARY

Appliqué — A cutout fabric shape that is secured to a larger background. Also refers to the technique of securing the cutout pieces.

Backing — The back or bottom layer of a quilt, sometimes called the "lining."

Backstitch — A reinforcing stitch taken at the beginning and end of a seam to secure stitches.

Basting — Large running stitches used to temporarily secure pieces or layers of fabric together. Basting is removed after permanent stitching.

Batting — The middle layer of a quilt that provides the insulation and warmth as well as the thickness.

Bias — The diagonal (45° for true bias) grain of fabric in relation to crosswise or lengthwise grain (see **Fig. 62**).

Binding — The fabric strip used to enclose the raw edges of the layered and quilted quilt. Also refers to the technique of finishing quilt edges in this way.

Blindstitch — A method of hand sewing an opening closed so that it is invisible.

Border — Strips of fabric that are used to frame a quilt top.

Chain piecing — A machine-piecing method consisting of joining pairs of pieces one after the other by feeding them through the sewing machine without cutting the thread between the pairs.

Grain — The direction of the threads in woven fabric. "Crosswise grain" refers to the threads running from selvage to selvage. "Lengthwise grain" refers to the threads running parallel to the selvages (**Fig. 62**).

Fig. 62

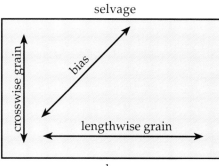

Machine baste — To baste using a sewing machine set at a long stitch length.

Miter — A method used to finish corners of quilt borders or bindings consisting of joining fabric pieces at a 45° angle.

Piecing — Sewing together the pieces of a quilt design to form a quilt block or an entire quilt top.

Pin basting — Using rust-proof safety pins to secure the layers of a quilt together prior to machine quilting.

Quilt block — Pieced or appliquéd sections that are sewn together to form a quilt top.

Quilt top — The decorative part of a quilt that is layered on top of the batting and backing.

Quilting — The stitching that holds together the 3 quilt layers (top, batting, and backing); or, the entire process of making a quilt.

Running stitch — A series of straight stitches with the stitch length equal to the space between stitches (**Fig. 63**).

Fig. 63

Sashing — Strips or blocks of fabric that separate individual blocks in a quilt top.

Seam allowance — The distance between the seam and the cut edge of the fabric. In quilting, the seam allowance is usually 1/4".

Selvages — The 2 finished lengthwise edges of fabric (see **Fig. 62**). Selvages should be trimmed from fabric before cutting.

Set (or Setting) — The arrangement of the quilt blocks as they are sewn together to form the quilt top.

Setting squares — Squares of plain (unpieced) fabric set between pieced or appliquéd quilt blocks in a quilt top.

Setting triangles — Triangles of fabric used around the outside of a diagonally-set quilt top to fill in between outer squares and border or binding.

Stencil — A pattern used for marking quilting lines.

Straight grain — The crosswise or lengthwise grain of fabric (see **Fig. 62**). The lengthwise grain has the least amount of stretch.

Strip set — Two or more strips of fabric that are sewn together along the long edges and then cut apart across the width of the sewn strips to create smaller units.

Triangle-square — In piecing, 2 right triangles joined along their long sides to form a square with a diagonal seam (**Fig. 64**).

Fig. 64

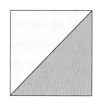

Unit — A pieced section that is made as individual steps in the quilt construction process are completed. Units are usually combined to make blocks or other sections of the quilt top.

CREDITS

We want to extend a warm *thank you* to the generous people who allowed us to photograph our projects at their homes.

- *Pineapple Quilt* (cover photo): Dr. Tony Johnson
- *Tree of Life Collection*: Duncan and Nancy Porter
- *Star of Bethlehem Collection*: Mr. and Mrs. James M. Adams
- *Four Seasons Collection:* Duncan and Nancy Porter
- *Plaid Garden*: Dr. Tony Johnson
- *Nine-Patch Mantel Scarf*: Dr. and Mrs. Richard Calhoun
- *Basket Collection*: Duncan and Nancy Porter
- *True Heart Wall Hanging*: Duncan and Nancy Porter
- *Little Quilts*: John and Anne Childs
- *Haunting Collection*: Duncan and Nancy Porter
- *Bachelor's Puzzle Collection*: Carl and Monte Brunck and Dr. and Mrs. David Smith
- *Starry Path*: Dr. Dan and Sandra Cook
- *Lady of the Lake Collection*: Duncan and Nancy Porter

We wish to thank The Empress of Little Rock Bed and Breakfast of Little Rock, Arkansas, for allowing us to photograph our Floral Nine-Patch and Broken Dishes quilts at the inn.

We also extend our thanks to Pinnacle Vista Lodge of Little Rock, Arkansas, for allowing us to photograph our Square Dance and Pineapple quilts at the lodge.

The following projects are from the collection of Bryce and Donna Hamilton, Minneapolis, Minnesota: Star of Bethlehem quilt and wall hanging, pages 18-20; Square Dance quilt, page 32; True Heart wall hanging, page 69; and Starry Path quilt, page 118.

The Lady of the Lake quilt on page 132 was designed by Sharon LoMonaco.

To Magna IV Color Imaging of Little Rock, Arkansas, we say thank you for the superb color reproduction and excellent pre-press preparation.

We especially want to thank photographers Mark Mathews, Larry Pennington, Karen Shirey, and Ken West of Peerless Photography, Little Rock, Arkansas, and Jerry R. Davis of Jerry Davis Photography, Little Rock, Arkansas, for their time, patience, and excellent work.

We extend a sincere *thank you* to all the people who assisted in making and testing the projects in this book: Janice Adams, Karen Call, Deborah B. Chance, Cindy Davis, Stephanie Fite, Wanda Fite, Patricia Galas, Genny Garrett, Judith H. Hassed, Judith M. Kline, Barbara Middleton, Gazelle Mode, Karen Sharp, Ruby Solida, Glenda Taylor, and Patricia Wiest; members of the Gardner Memorial United Methodist Church, North Little Rock, Arkansas: Elois Allain, Maxie Bramblett, Alice Dong, Vina Lendermon, Fredda McBride, Betty Smith, Esther Starkey, and Thelma Starkey; and members of the Mabelvale United Methodist Church, Mabelvale, Arkansas: Sunny Ball, Mary Sue Meyers, Carolyn Moseley, Mickey Riddle, and Jacquelynn Spann.